# THE CRICKET COAC
# MAN MANAGEMENT

CW00456928

# The Cricket Coach's Guide to Man Management

David Roberts

NOTTINGHAM
University Press

Nottingham University Press
Manor Farm, Main Street, Thrumpton
Nottingham, NG11 0AX, United Kingdom

NOTTINGHAM

First published 2000

**British Library Cataloguing in Publication Data**
The Cricket Coach's Guide to Man Management
Roberts, D.E.

ISBN    1-897676-93-X

Typeset by Nottingham University Press, Nottingham
Printed and bound by The Cromwell Press, Trowbridge, Wiltshire

# CONTENTS

# Acknowledgements

I am grateful to all the cricket coaches who have attended the Bradford course, and particularly to the following cricketers, coaches, and administrators, who have contributed so much – knowingly or otherwise – to the contents of this book.

Bob Appleyard, formerly of England and Yorkshire County Cricket Club; Bill Athey, Head Coach, Worcestershire County Cricket Club; Jack Birkenshaw, Head Coach, Leicestershire County Cricket Club; Damian D'Oliveira, Assistant Coach, Worcestershire County Cricket Club; John Emburey, Independent cricket coach, formerly England and Middlesex; Paul Farbrace, National Coach, England and Wales Cricket Board; Mike Hendrick, National Coach, Scottish Cricket Union; Paul Johnson, Senior Player, Nottinghamshire County Cricket Club; Gordon Lord, National Coaching Scheme Co-ordinator, England and Wales Cricket Board; Hugh Morris, Technical Director, England and Wales Cricket Board; Mick Newell, Nottinghamshire County Cricket Club; Steve Oldham, Cricket Development Officer, Yorkshire County Cricket Club; Clive Rice, Coach, Nottinghamshire County Cricket Club; Steve Rhodes, senior player and wicket keeper, Worcestershire County Cricket Club; Robin Smith, Captain 1st XI, Hampshire County Cricket Club; Rev Mike Vockins, Secretary, Worcestershire County Cricket Club; Steve Watkin, Senior Player, Glamorgan County Cricket Club; Simon Willis, Cricket Administration Manager, Kent County Cricket Club; Tony Wright, senior player, Gloucestershire County Cricket Club, and Peter Wynne-Thomas, cricket historian, Nottinghamshire County Cricket Club.

Thanks are also due to Dr R Meredith Belbin, Belbin Associates, for kind permission to use material from his Interplace system and quotations from his book Team Roles at Work; to Wendy Lord, independent consultant, formerly Chief Psychologist, ASE, for her encouragement and constructive comments. To The Institute of Personality and Ability Testing, Inc., and NFER – NELSON Publishing Company Ltd., for permission to reproduce the 16PF Profile Sheet.

To Patsy, for her support and for keeping the coffee flowing. Finally, to my colleagues and visiting tutors at the University of Bradford Management Centre, Steve Browning, independent consultant, and Michael Fordham, independent consultant and former sports coach. Without Michael, the Bradford cricket coach's course would not have developed as successfully as it has...

# Introduction

When the irresistible force meets the immovable object unusual things can happen. And so it was that the pressures which led to the creating of the Coaching and Management Development Programme at the University of Bradford Management Centre were the result of a number of irresistible forces creating one seemingly immovable object – the world of cricket.

On a practical level the Programme was simply a course designed to improve the skills of county coaches. However, the range of skills was deliberately innovative and focused on the soft skills of management, coupled with an understanding of the business of the game of cricket, intended to establish a group of senior coaches who would make a significant contribution to the continued professionalisation of the game.

Time will tell whether the long-term aspirations will be met. Certainly the initial expectations have been far exceeded and the course has succeeded in producing a group of nearly fifty county coaches and senior players who have one thing in common – the 'Bradford Experience'.

Where it all started and how it came to be that the then TCCB decided that a business school could help in the process is intriguing and worthy of explanation. My part in that process became the one continuous thread that linked different individuals, organisations and institutions into a scheme whose outcomes continue to ripple outwards and in ever widening and overlapping circles.

The 'Bradford Experience' group has grown to include the National Coaches; one of its number is the Technical Director of the England and Wales Cricket Board, elements of the programme are embodied in Level III of the new National Coaching Scheme, and in future those aspiring to Level IV will be subject to a formal assessment of these key elements. The body of knowledge accumulated by and with the programme delegates continues to grow and is now being used to further advise improvement in cricket coaching – this book is testament to that.

In 1999 the University of Bradford led a consortium bid with Bradford College, Leeds University and Leeds Metropolitan University and became one of only 6 ECB accredited University Centres of Cricketing Excellence.

One of the elements of the bid that encouraged and enabled that accreditation was the availability to the Bradford/Leeds consortium of the Bradford Park Avenue Cricket Ground. The ground was made available in more ways than one through the good offices of the Trustees of the YCC Charity Trust and in particular one of its trustees – former Yorkshire and England bowler, Bob Appleyard.

It was indeed at Bradford Park Avenue where the story of our Programme began.

I had recently begun working with Bradford Management Centre and had been pleasantly surprised to be asked to lend some marketing effort to the Graduates Association – they were planning a benefit match at Bradford Park Avenue, a One-Day International between Pakistan and the West Indies.

On making inquiries it emerged that the man I needed to contact was Bob Appleyard who had played a key role in the re-establishment of the grounds as a First Class County ground which was home to the Yorkshire Academy. He soon demonstrated his single-mindedness and devotion to the improvement of the game by suggesting that we meet to discuss how the University could help, probably by providing educational support for young players.

Over the next few months he cajoled, persisted and eventually persuaded Lord's to taken an interest. In the meantime there was a regular visit with some interested parties ranging from Dennis Silk to Ray Illingworth and including Frank 'Typhoon' Tyson who had travelled from Australia where he had experienced the benefits of such an idea.

Eventually the debate began to take shape; Phil Neale, Tim Lamb and Micky Stewart attended a meeting, and the focus of attention became coaches, current or aspiring, at County level.

Micky Stewart who was the Director of Coaching and Excellence became the product champion while I worked with a group of enthusiastic academics who had admitted their love for the game of cricket. Everyone was keen to contribute - Brian Gilding with the programme design, Stuart Sanderson with the case study and Michael Fordham bringing his team to bear on the soft skills and interpersonal expertise. All encouraged by the then Director, David Weir who donned a mortarboard with his cricket whites to grace the cover of the University magazine.

Not only had the idea caught the imagination at Lord's, it had unleashed the native enthusiasm of the faculty and tutors, who have worked with the programme since the beginning and others who have helped along the way.

The resulting course had one representative from each of the first class counties ranging from coach, to senior player. The basic elements were two modules in Bradford, each one-week long. The first concentrated on the soft skills and the second on the business of the game - finance, marketing and strategy.

The case study - Westshire Cricket Club - had profit and loss accounts, problems with the overseas player and a whole range of issues that linked learning points to the cricket world of the delegates. The emphasis was on applied learning and it worked. The series led by Michael Fordham and the team of Steve Browning and David Roberts created insight and introduced a framework for debate which generated animated discussions – the group moulded together sharing ideas and personal experiences which made the sessions invaluable. As always the Course Administrator, Dorothy Michell organised the team and delegates.

A 2-day refresher and pre-season preparation of a personal development plan followed the residentials for each delegate. During the season some of the tutors managed a little 'pastoral support' visiting the delegates on home territory, usually when there was some cricket. This meant that we could meet two delegates from different counties at the same time and it was obvious from the feedback and the exceptional level of interest from the County Chairman and Chief Executive that they were keen to nominate potential candidates for another intake the following year.

In further discussion it was agreed that an advanced module would follow a review after the season and the shape of the programme was fixed.

The specific content continued to change in response to group discussion and a whole range of outside speakers added to the richness of the experience.

Steve Backley gave a session on preparation in the world of athletics, Mike Brearley made a rare appearance to discuss captaincy, Gary Tasker, Chief Executive of Bradford Bulls shared his experience in a sport going through radical change, dominated by Australian coaches, and Bill Ainsworth told us how he had been the architect responsible for the innovative planned development of Durham's new County ground at the Riverside Stadium. Dave Gilbert actually gave the Australian perspective.

The reviews from delegates were, and continue to be, exceptional – comments included "I wish I'd been on this course when I was a captain – I might still have been", to a county cricket executive who wanted to know how a slightly older coach had the temerity to argue finances with the club's treasurer.

It was all a very long way from what Bob Appleyard had in mind and yet it was an important element of the same process – to improve the game. It would not have happened without his foresight and tenacity (some would call it bloody-mindedness – in the nicest possible way).

And so it was that when I called him to let him know that the Bradford/Leeds bid to become a University Centre of Cricketing Excellence had been successful it seemed as though it had been possible to fulfil his original aspirations – to provide an opportunity for young gifted cricketers to pursue a University course and to maintain the highest level of cricket coaching, training and competition at Bradford Park Avenue.

Robert McClements
Chairman, Executive Development Programme
and Director of the ECB Coaching and Management
Development Programme, Bradford University

# Author's note

The objective of this book is not only to reflect some of the Bradford course content but also to present some of the findings of sport and general psychology researchers, and to make them accessible to cricket coaches. Cricket has generated more literature than any other sport, but much less is published dealing with the management skills that a coach at any level is likely to need. There are many which offer the injunction to 'understand your players', and 'communicate' with them, not to mention demonstrating 'leadership', but most of these books are long on advocacy and short on how to do it. This book aims to fill that gap. Much of the content is as relevant to other sports as to cricket, and I have therefore used examples from other sports to illustrate a point where appropriate.

I have kept technical jargon to the minimum, but some is necessary. Interpersonal skills and some other aspects of psychology are frequently spoken of in a condescending way as being 'vague' or by some other similar derogatory expression. Some concepts may seem to be rather abstract, and that is where we need to use specific words and explain clearly their meanings. The skills of management, of coaching, and of captaincy are sometimes referred to as 'soft skills'. In fact the soft skills can be quite hard to put into practice, and the so-called 'hard skills' – the technical skills - are perhaps easier.

I hope that those who wish to progress to the higher levels of coaching will find this book of value and perhaps it may also act as a spur to those who wish to acquire deeper knowledge in areas they find particularly interesting.

David Roberts
Spring, 2000

# 1    Interpreting other people's behaviour

*Then there's Lord's with its crowded Pavilion,*
*"Well fielded", "Well bowled," and "Well played";*
*The chaff when a wide is delivered,*
*And cheers when a good hit is made.*

*Then There's Lord's*
Anon

When Nasser Hussain was appointed England's cricket captain in 1999 the first thing he did was to recall two cricketers previously labelled as "difficult", and "hard to handle". Andy Caddick and Phil Tuffnell, arguably two of the best bowlers in the country, had been ignored by previous captains. Caddick's loot of 105 county wickets in 1998 was not enough to take him to Australia that winter. South Africa's coach, Bob Woolmer, writing in a Sunday newspaper, said:

> *"My experience of dealing with so-called problem players has convinced me that 'eccentricity' should not be a bar to selection." He went on: "In all my dealings with Peter Pollock, the convenor of the South African selectors, his approach was that the best players should be picked and then it was down to the captain and the coach to make those who were considered difficult, part of the team on and off the field."*

The job of the sports coach is essentially that of dealing with other people. It may be no exaggeration to say that the technical aspects of sport – any sport - are in fact the easiest to get to grips with. The principles will be well known, there will be many players to whom one can look for excellent examples of how the game should be played, and there will be no shortage of advice from keen observers of the game.

Something which is far more difficult for the coach, and which is usually given scant attention in cricket coaching books, is the need to understand the players in order to get the best out of them. Some people feel that they are able to understand others easily enough.

They may think on the lines that since they have been dealing with fellow human beings all their lives, they have become quite good at it. They may be very instinctive people who have learned to trust their own judgement. Certainly some are better at it than others, but all of us at times, can be surprised by the behaviour of other people – even those we know well. "I wouldn't have believed it," we might say when someone acts out of character. And perhaps even more frequently, "I just *don't* understand him."

The purpose of this chapter therefore, is to try to highlight some of the principles that the cricket coach needs to be aware of, if he aspires to understand others. You're probably thinking: it's all very well saying that we need to understand people, but *how do we actually do it*? Well, there are principles in general psychology that we can apply. These principles can be understood without getting bogged down in too many technical terms; the intention here is to give the reader pointers that will help him to try to understand others. Where the use of technical terms is unavoidable, they will be explained.

In my consultancy work using psychometric tests, I will usually be hired by an organisation, (the client) to provide insights about existing or potential staff (the candidates). I administer a battery of tests, explaining the background to each and eventually providing feedback to the candidate as well as the client. The test battery provides much information that could not reasonably be gained through normal interview. The tests deal with personality, interpersonal relationships, and approaches to teamwork, as well as mental abilities. After spending say two or three hours with a candidate, and quickly scanning the test results prior to a more detailed inspection, I feel I know a little more about him or her than I did at the outset. The client, however, may well have a more optimistic view, and if I feel unable to answer his queries about the candidate with a confident and full reply, he might very well think – "Look, you've spent a *whole morning* with this candidate. You must know all about him, surely." But which of us would like to feel that another person has comprehensive knowledge about us after just a few hours' acquaintance? We may even feel we don't completely understand members of our own family. Or ourselves. An Oscar Wilde character said, "I am the only person in the world I should like to know thoroughly," and many of us might feel the same.

To continue the example above, my client might say, "What did you think of his personality?" or "I think I can tell from his behaviour that he'll settle into the job quite well," or "He's got an odd attitude",

What do we mean by these words – personality, behaviour, and attitude?

Are they interchangeable, in fact? In common language they certainly are, but they actually have somewhat different meanings to psychologists.

We live in times when the personality, behaviour and attitudes of others are constantly examined and discussed – in newspapers, magazines, on television and radio. We seem obsessed with the behaviour of other people, and nowhere is this more obvious than in the world of entertainment – and sport in particular. It seems that almost every well-known sportsman is the subject, at some time, of several columns inches of newsprint at the very least, speculating about some aspect of his personality, and in turn most sportsmen seem happy to write about the personalities of those with whom they have played. In sport the behaviour of teams as well as of individuals, is apparent for all to see. Unfortunately much of the comment is sensationalised if not downright inaccurate, but the public's appetite for so-called "insights" into the personalities of the famous seems to be insatiable, and the supply therefore, is never-ending.

So let's look at personality, behaviour, and attitude, try to determine what we mean by each, and identify general principles likely to be helpful to the cricket coach.

## Personality

Man's recorded interest in the notion of personality goes back to at least 400 BC. As usual, the Greeks had a word (or words) for it - they attempted to define personality and labelled people as sanguine (energetic), phlegmatic (sluggish and apathetic), choleric (irritable), and melancholic (depressive). These are temperaments and are generally regarded as the more stable elements of personality.

We talk of television personalities; of those with a weak personality, or a strong one; we even talk of people with no personality. We are quick to classify people according to some perceived personality trait. We believe that Yorkshiremen are blunt, Scots are mean, the Welsh garrulous, the French logical, the Germans meticulous. This easy labeling creates stereotypes. We may actually know very little about such people, but we don't let that get in the way of the facts, nor of what we think of as a good description of their personality! These "common sense" theories are sometimes called *implicit* personality theories.

Here is a list of some personality trait labels of two cricketers:

    (a) reserved
    (b) anxious
    (c) dominant
    (d) tough minded
    (e) bold
    (f) forthright
    (g) shy
    (h) imaginative
    (i) impulsive
    (j) serious.

Try to identify which characteristics are likely to hang together for each of the two players. Although you won't know the people concerned, you will probably have little difficulty in doing this.

Most people would identify the two sets as being (a), (b), (g), (h), (j) and (c), (d), (e) (f) and (i). However there is no reason why someone who is reserved cannot be confident as well; no reason why an anxious person should not be bold. One of the major personality assessments in use today, The Sixteen Personality Factor Questionnaire (16PF5)[1] which has been used extensively by sport psychologists, features 16 personality characteristics, each of which has a scale from 1 – 10. (See Appendix 1.)The mathematically minded reader may like to know that there can be 10 quadrillion combinations (10 to the 16th power), representing 10 possible scores on each of the 16 primary scales. I have been using this assessment for more than 20 years and during that time I have probably seen about five thousand of the possible profiles. Although some combinations will be rare, all are feasible.

Given this bewildering variety of personality combinations, the coach might feel daunted at the prospect of trying to understand his players. Fortunately there are some principles that an astute coach can learn and use to identify some personality characteristics. We shall deal with these a little later in this chapter.

We tend to regard our personalities as private, something intrinsically "us". This may explain why some people are rather wary of undertaking a personality test. They feel that their essential "self" is being invaded. However, it is not about being assessed or not being assessed, because we all assess each other all the time: it is about being assessed fairly, competently, and professionally, rather than perhaps, unfairly, casually, and badly.

Our personality traits are usually stable over much of our lives, and in many different situations. We have a *disposition* to behave in a certain way, and it is this consistency of behaviour that enables us to predict how others will behave in given situations. If there were no consistency the concept of personality would vanish, and we would be at a loss to describe friends and colleagues to those who don't know them.

We say that this consistency enables us to predict how others will behave. This is true – but only up to a point, because if it were true all the time and in all situations our behaviour would appear very rigid. A moment's thought will clarify this. Do we behave in the same manner in the presence of a member of our family as with a close friend? With our boss at work and with someone whom we have never met before? With a cricketer new to the team, as with an experienced and senior player? Clearly not. It is the flexibility in our behaviour that enables us to relate appropriately to different people. We "read" a situation and then behave in a manner we think appropriate.

Looking at it from another perspective, we tend to believe that most people behave consistently. A useful example is that of a television newscaster. He or she will appear to be formal; behaviour whilst broadcasting will be predictable; the manner will be serious, apart from a tight smile perhaps at the end of the broadcast. We are shocked therefore if we hear that the same person was involved in an unseemly public argument, or was accused of ill-treating a child or an animal. We are very familiar with these characters and because they behave in the same way every time we see them, we mistakenly believe that they might behave like that in other situations. We use our implicit personality theory to focus on a few characteristics and then fill in the blanks to arrive at a conclusion. If we were to think about it properly, we would realise the shortcomings of this approach, but our casual, uncritical thinking misleads us.

There are other factors to challenge the concept of our personalities being consistent. For example many individual characteristics remain constant, such as our gestures, our appearance, and the way in which we speak. Because these are constant, we believe that personality is constant also. A further tendency is for us to rely on descriptions of personality to judge a situation, rather than looking at the situation itself. It is estimated that we have around 17–18,000 words to describe aspects of personality, so there is no shortage of words at our command. We have far fewer words with which to label situations, and therefore it is easier to classify the person rather than situation.

We might therefore say that a person is difficult or unco-operative, rather than make the effort to describe the situation in which that person finds him or her self.

We have said that it is important for the coach to understand his players and one way to do this is to focus on the thinking preferences that a player might have. These preferences are the result of an unconscious decision-making process on our part[2]. In the same way that we did not decide to be left- or right-handed, so we did not make a *conscious decision* to be introvert or extravert. At some point in our development, and in dealing with the world around us, we simply decided to prefer one method than the other.

## Action-centred people

One of the more obvious features of personality is that of extraversion and introversion. The majority of people are familiar with these terms, which form two of our most identifiable personality characteristics. Many of us believe we know what constitutes an extravert - an easy going, sociable type of person, perhaps with plenty to say, and easy to get to know. The clue to identification perhaps lies in the last comment - that of being easy to get to know. Perhaps that is one reason why extraverts appear to be more popular than are introverts. They seem more "up-front", more interesting, even exciting. To use the current phrase, we have no difficulty in "knowing where they are coming from." Extraverts are more likely to enjoy meeting other people, and they will be more "transparent" in the sense that others are more likely to know what they are thinking. They are freer with their opinions, and they will see little point in reflecting about things, being much more prone to action.

## Reflective people

These are more likely to be introverted – to a greater or lesser extent of course. If personality characteristics are spread evenly amongst the population, we ought to find as many introverts as extraverts. But we don't. It is the one personality factor that has a skewed distribution with approximately 70% being extravert (to varying degrees of course) and 30% being introvert, again to varying degrees.

So extraverts are generally popular, introverts perhaps less so. Why should this be? The answer lies almost certainly in the difficulty of getting to know them.

Whereas an extravert is very largely focused on the outside world, - what is going on around him - the introvert's focus is inward looking, and it will therefore be more difficult to get know him. The best way to get to know an introvert is to find out what his deeper interests might be, for he will almost certainly have some. *If an introvert is simply taken at face value his abilities are likely to be underestimated.*

From time to time, every cricket coach will face the task of trying to get to know someone who is rather quiet, even withdrawn. A coach has to understand what makes such a person "tick" and he may not be able to improve a player's performance significantly, until he can gain that person's confidence and begin to understand what might motivate him. Introverts like to reflect on a problem before committing themselves; they may be relatively quiet during meetings, and there is always the risk that they may be prone to what Belbin calls "paralysis by analysis."

Because introversion and extraversion are important and perhaps the most readily identifiable personal characteristics, we shall look at another example that illustrates the difference between the two. Introversion and extraversion are about a particular type of energy. Introverts find their energy from their inner world of ideas, concepts, and abstractions. Because they have a rich inner life, they seem to require less from the outside world. Extraverts find their energy from their involvement with the world around them. They will spend less time on thought than will the introvert because they are attracted to external realities. Clearly, extreme introverts and extraverts can be identified readily. But of course many people will fall in the middle range, and may be a little more difficult to identify. From these clues, the coach may realise that the quieter cricketer may be interested in theories and the technical principles of cricket, whilst the more extravert will prefer practical demonstrations and action. The introvert will look inward to pursue fewer interests more deeply and is likely to take a more reflective approach to learning. The extravert is more likely to learn from practical examples, and is alert to external events i.e. outside himself.

Another illustration may help to highlight the differences – and potential problems - between introverts and extraverts.

An extravert cricketer arrived home after a very hard day, to be greeted by his wife who reminded him that they had accepted an invitation to go to a dinner function where he will be expected to make an amusing speech. "More rubber chicken," he groaned. He really wanted to stay in for once. The introverted wife also wanted to stay in, but they had promised to attend, so off they went. They had almost nothing to say to each other on the journey.

On arriving at the dinner they were greeted by old friends, acquaintances and former teammates, and within minutes the extravert husband was happily chatting to people, as enthusiastic as ever. He very soon forgot his tiredness, enjoyed the small talk, and made a very amusing speech after dinner.

On the way home, the introverted wife indicated that she was deeply unhappy. She said "How can those people, with their silly chatter turn you on so much? I'm your wife. What's so special about them?" They thought their marriage was in trouble because neither fully understood the preferences and motivations of the other.

### What to look for in Action-centred – Reflective People

For an action-centred person – an extravert - there is "no impression without expression." In other words, they feel compelled to talk about anything which has made an impression on them. Extraverts will need to talk about new experiences, about the book they have just read, the film they have seen, what happened in the office or in the dressing room. The introvert will not feel the need to talk about such things as a matter of course. They are less important. Look for quieter, even withdrawn players, who are more likely to be interested in theories. They may have fewer interests than the extravert, but may pursue them at a deeper level.

### "Concrete" thinkers

Some people prefer to learn largely through facts, and this can be very relevant to a cricketer's learning style. Such people pay attention both to what they read and what they observe. They like detail. They prefer to take a pragmatic approach to problem solving. "Has it worked before?" they might ask. They are concerned with the realities of a situation, and they tend to be impatient with "hunches" and ideas that have not been properly thought through. They are likely to prefer literal meanings and concrete experiences. So they may pay close attention to what is said and they will be reliant on facts and hard data.

## Ideas people

Others may be stronger in the generation of ideas. They are able to "take a helicopter view" of a problem; they will enjoy a brainstorming approach to problems; they can make a mental jump from one idea to another (unrelated) idea; they can see possibilities, and patterns in situations. They may rely on their "sixth sense". They may still use the data which the concrete thinker will use, but they will also be able to "read between the lines" to arrive at their judgement. They are likely to be interested in theories and principles as a means to understanding something.

---

### What to look for in concrete thinkers – ideas people

Strong concrete thinkers are interested in facts, which they will analyse objectively. They pay regard to hard data and facts – whether in written, verbal, or visual form. Ideas people will enjoy those things that stimulate their imagination and require them to look at possibilities. They will be looking for patterns of activity, looking at facts, but filling in the blanks with their own reading of a situation.

---

## Logical people

In arriving at a decision, people who are strong logical thinkers will view a problem impersonally and use their analytical skills to arrive at their solution. They are able to detach themselves from a situation and look at it objectively. They are likely to be task-centred, putting the job in hand before considerations about the people. They are likely to be convinced primarily by logical argument. They like to link cause and effect.

## "Values" people

A person with strong values will tend to override the logical aspects and focus on personal issues — what they feel to be intrinsically and morally "right". They may still look at a situation logically, but they will modify their decision according to how it might impinge on their sense of values. Such people are likely to be able to get along with others more readily than most. To illustrate the Logical – Values concept, cast your mind back to the eighties when Margaret Thatcher was Prime Minister, and Neil Kinnock was Leader of the Opposition. At Question Time, you will have almost certainly heard something like this:

KINNOCK: Has the Honourable Lady no compassion? Does she not realise that about 20% of the housing in this country is sub-standard?

THATCHER: Could I suggest to the Honourable Member that if he purports to be a future Prime Minister of this country he should first get his facts right? The figure is not 20% as he states, but 14%.

The figures and the example above are of course fictitious, but they serve to make the point that whilst one person relies on facts (nothing wrong with that), the other person relies on an inner sense of values almost regardless of the facts (nothing wrong with that either). They are simply different ways of looking at the world. The more we are able to understand the other's point of view, the better we will be able to shape our own response to it. Transferring that to the learning situation, value-centred people are more likely to commit to relationships and harmony with peers and coaches.

---

### What to look for in logical – values people

Those who prefer to make decisions using their preference for logical thinking tend to rely on reason. They will analyse a situation, and may use a step-by-step approach from cause to effect. This is not to say that they have no "feelings" – it is simply that they will concentrate on the logicality or otherwise of a situation. Those with a preference for Values are likely to consider the human implications of a decision first, and they are likely to do this even if the facts of a situation seem to call for a logical approach.

---

## Orderly people

This refers to being organised, decisive and systematic. Learners with preferences in this will prefer to "know where they stand" and to have clear plans. They do not like meetings that end with no firm conclusions; they are likely to be decisive and prefer an organised approach to life; they will feel uneasy unless they have been able to prepare properly; they will believe in a degree of regulation and control.

## Spontaneous people

These people prefer to leave their options open, being curious, flexible and tolerant. They will probably leave work until the last minute. They like spontaneity, and they are prepared to adapt. They like to keep an open mind.

### What to look for in orderly – spontaneous people

A preference for orderliness can be identified by a desire to have things wrapped up; timings and dates will be important; they will not like loose ends. A preference for spontaneity will be shown by a desire not to be tied; to be prepared to leave all options open until the last minute if necessary; to be flexible and to do things on the spur of the moment.

Now that we have outlined these preferences, we can see how a particular pattern of individual preferences may be combined.

Try to identify the possible personality preferences of one of your players. You will then be able to work out his other strengths and possible areas for development, and if this is used with discretion, it could enable you to not only understand your players better, but to be able to identify how they might best learn. Unfortunately we assume that everyone learns in the same way, but this is far from the truth. Some people learn by reading and following instructions, and by trying to understand the underlying theory; whilst others are more concerned with "getting on with it", putting something into practice and learning as they go along.

## Behaviour

So what of behaviour? Psychologists use the word to refer to everything we do, which is observable. For our purposes, this includes that which we do consciously – gesticulating, speaking, nodding – in fact the whole range of behaviour we use in our dealings with others. Our behaviour is what other people see of us, and it is therefore important that it reflects what we truly want it to reflect. This may seem an obvious point, but frequently most of us don't consciously organise our behaviour as well as we might. Others therefore misunderstand us. They misunderstand us because our behaviour is not reflecting our real thoughts, attitudes and feelings. In computer-speak we refer to WYSIWYG (what you see is what you get), but when we deal with others, what we see may be *all* that we get, but it may not reflect what the individual is thinking or feeling. We are therefore in danger of picking up the wrong message.

In addition to this, psychologists have shown that to a large extent, our observable behaviour determines the other person's reactions. We smile; the other person smiles back; we nod in agreement and the other person is encouraged to be more forthcoming. (If you doubt this, watch a television interview closely.)

You may wonder how our behaviour is determined. The easiest way to describe this is to imagine your self-concept or self-image, to be at the centre of a circle (Figure 1). That represents what you believe about yourself – good or bad, competent or otherwise, determined or irresolute and so on. We are dealing here with your set of inner beliefs about yourself. Your self-concept will in turn determine your feelings. Your feelings in turn determine your behaviour, although this is not always the case, because we are not always honest with others or ourselves.

For example, we may take a dislike to a new boss, but be careful not to show this in our behaviour – at least initially. We realise that it would be tactful to keep our view to ourselves. Some may regard this as being insincere, others as being diplomatic. It gives rise to the question as to whether you are really being yourself or whether you are simply responding to a situation. If you respond to each situation in a different manner, how will others know which is the real you? Some people are remarkably good at concealing their real feelings and manage to divulge very little about themselves even to those who have known them for some time. Whilst they are excellent diplomats, people may wonder what they are really thinking, and they

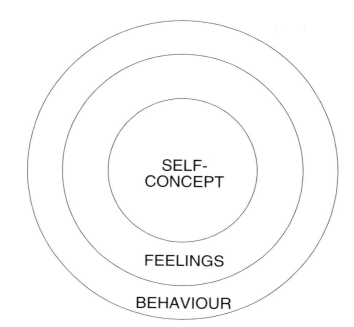

**Figure 1**
The relationship
between self
concept, feelings
and behaviour

probably want to know this so that they can regulate and adjust their own behaviour accordingly. Some might be very direct. They say what they think with little regard to the impact that might have on others. Such people are usually seen as being warm. Their colleagues might be reassured and say, "you know where you are with him," although their tactlessness may create difficulties.

## Attitude

Many years ago judo was my sport and in my part of the country we had one of the most promising lightweights at that time. He was a genial, outgoing sort of person, easy to get along with, and unfailingly cheerful. The area coach spotted his potential early on, and had given him many hours of one-to-one coaching. He was light on his feet, a fast mover, and powerful for his weight. We were all convinced that Danny could be an international. There was only one problem: his attitude. He was a fun-loving sort of chap and just couldn't knuckle down to the serious training that was required if he was to represent his country. Everything was something of a joke to him. Perhaps too much talent is a disadvantage, because success can come too easily

– and because it came too easily, Danny had not learned to cope with failure. He made the area team easily – without the need to train hard. Getting beyond that was tougher. He entered for the national trials but was beaten. He didn't want it badly enough and we realised that he didn't have the right *attitude*.

So what do we mean by attitude? It seems that it can mean almost anything that we want it to mean; people use the word very loosely in everyday speech, and use it as a label for a variety of beliefs, emotions, and behaviour. Our attitudes are often expressed in the form of an opinion: I dislike politicians; I love cricket and football; I like a good novel.

However, the behaviour that we observe and label as an attitude, is conditioned by *our own attitude*. In the example of Danny the judo player, I saw his attitude as being very carefree and inappropriate for someone attending trials for the national team. Someone else, not directly concerned with the sport, might have interpreted his attitude quite differently. They might have said, "What's the problem? He's just a young lad enjoying his sport, isn't he? What's wrong with that?" And of course from a by-stander's point of view there was nothing at all wrong with that.

The side of ourselves that most of us show to the outside world is only a small part of our personality. Much is hidden beneath the surface. Yet if we are to understand those we work with, particularly members of our team, we need to have some method for getting to those hidden parts. We need some understanding of the mainsprings of human behaviour. We also need to understand ourselves. And our own prejudices.

Gary was applying for a job with a major car manufacturer. He came into the interview room in a somewhat slack manner. He had two earrings, longish hair, and a shirt open at the neck. A tattoo adorned each wrist. His manner was casual, and he slumped into the chair. Not an impressive way to start an interview, and one likely to stir the prejudices of most interviewers.

The employer was looking for a number of skills, amongst which was the ability to solve problems. When the candidate was asked whether he had solved any difficult problems at work in the last year or so, he replied that he hadn't – his repetitive, routine, factory job didn't require him to. The questioning therefore switched to his life outside work, in search of an appropriate example. As a prompt, he was asked what he would do if his car broke down. "Funny you should say that", he said, now appearing to be quite animated, "That happened only last week. I had a look at the engine and checked all the obvious things. They were OK so I guessed it was the timing that was out. I went off to the library and got the Haynes manual for my car, and took the engine down that same afternoon. And I wasn't sure how many degrees before top dead centre, the piston had to be. But it was all in the manual. No problem, really…" He was away. Not only did he demonstrate that he could solve mechanical problems from his own knowledge, but more importantly, he knew where to go to add to his own knowledge. Although he did not behave like a more conventional candidate might do at an interview, there was no doubt that he was able to meet the company's requirements, at least with regard to problem solving. Although first impressions are important, this is so because few have been trained to ignore their prejudices until the other person has revealed sufficient of themselves for a balanced judgement to be formed. In this interview, a little patience and tolerance on the part of the interviewer enabled the candidate to demonstrate convincingly that he had at least one of the main characteristics that the employer was looking for.

And the connection with coaching? Coaching is an intensely personal relationship, and in order for that to develop naturally and blossom into something productive for both parties, we must avoid making snap judgements – favourable or unfavourable – about others. Jack Birkenshaw, formerly of Yorkshire and England and now Head Coach at Leicestershire says: *"I used to look at the skill factor alone. Now I make the effort get to know the chap much better."*

# CHECK LIST FOR INTERPRETING OTHERS' BEHAVIOUR

❖ The ability to interpret the behaviour of others is an important element in the work of the coach.

❖ We use the words personality, behaviour, and attitudes to describe other people.

❖ *Personality* refers to a set of traits or characteristics, which are reasonably stable over a period of time. However, we usually adapt our behaviour to suit particular circumstances.

❖ People express preferences for the way in which they make decisions and this can give important clues about the way in which they like to learn.

❖ Psychologists use the term *behaviour* to describe what we actually do, and which is therefore observable. Because our behaviour is all that others see of us, it is important that it reflects what we want it to reflect. If it does not, others may pick up the wrong signals, resulting in misunderstanding.

❖ Our *self-concept* or *self-image* determines our feelings and these in turn shape our behaviour. This may not always be the case however, since we are not always honest with ourselves or with others.

❖ *Attitude* is the word we use to describe a mixture of beliefs, emotions, and behaviour.

❖ Avoid making snap judgements about people.

# 2 Presenting yourself

*I was about eleven when I decided not to captain England and if I may say so I now regard that as a wise decision. At eleven I arrived at the grammar school which then plumped out its numbers by taking in boys from other small towns and villages in the neighbourhood. Some of them were good. Not that I was bad. I was dreadful. Always out in the first over, mostly at the first straight ball; always hurt my hands fielding; always bowled either to second slip or silly mid-on; always hoping that some miracle would turn me into Denis Compton. I used Brylcreem every day.*

On the Boundary
Melvyn Bragg

Some years ago I was a member of a governing body. We were each appointed by the Home Secretary, met monthly, and were available for people within the establishment to come and see us. We dressed reasonably soberly – business suit and tie for the men, women also wearing something appropriate. One day a new member, an academic, joined. He wore cheap looking trousers that were usually crumpled, with a tee shirt underneath a V-neck pullover. His manner was as casual as his dress, almost condescending. His analytical style of questioning and querying almost everything conveyed an impression of intellectual arrogance. He often made good contributions to the meeting, but I did not like him. Why? More than anything else, it was his dress, which I felt made a statement about his view of the committee – all of us. Perhaps also, it was that whilst the rest of us were somewhat proud to serve on the committee, he was almost certainly nominated on the 'Buggins' turn' principle. Although the era of more casual dressing had arrived by then, it was still not the sort of meeting in which to turn up in tee shirt and pullover. Of course there were no written standards as to what we should wear, there was no imposition of that sort. But there was an implicit understanding that you dressed in normal business clothes. None of us ever discussed his dress or anything else about him, but I am sure that others felt the same as I did. He never really fitted in and he resigned after a year or so.

But of course dress is just one of the many ways in which we convey impressions of ourselves to others. Most of us present ourselves in a manner that we believe fits the nature of the occasion, whatever that might be. The sociologist Erving Goffman[1] said, "Each individual entering a conversation projects by dress, manner and opening remarks a proposal for the basis of what the interaction shall be." This can be almost anything you want it to be – a meeting of equals, teacher to student, coach to player, boss to subordinate. Once having established this relationship, you need to maintain it. The cricket coach is as much a manager as any in industry or commerce, and the same unwritten rules apply. The coach will need to maintain some dignity (but avoiding pomposity at all costs) and to put a little distance between himself and his players. If he does not do this, and tries to adopt an over-friendly attitude, he runs the risk of not being taken seriously. It is particularly difficult for the coach whose players are well known to him. Every newly appointed manager has the task of treading a very fine dividing line between being one of the group (which he was), and a part of the management (which he is).

We are told that first impressions count – and they most certainly do, since to correct a first impression at a later date may be difficult. The other person will have already formed a view of you, and many people are reluctant to change their original impressions. Any subsequent information, which conflicts with first impressions, is likely to be ignored or distorted. Nowhere is this more apparent than in the conventional interview – "I knew within the first minute of him coming into the room, that he was not for us." Most of us will have heard comments such as that, and many of us will also be guilty of making them. As we saw in the last chapter, those who have been trained in interviewing techniques will have learned to postpone such judgements until sufficient evidence about overall suitability has been accumulated. They will then carefully weigh that evidence before coming to a conclusion.

But the interview is a special, indeed an artificial, situation, and one in which both parties are likely to project the behaviour that they think will best serve their purpose – most certainly a 'performance' in Goffman's sense of the word. In our working and social lives we have countless meetings – both casual and formal – and each one is an opportunity for us to project an image that is appropriate to the situation. Does that sound devious? Maybe.

## Body language

Many of us are surprised when those we know well misinterpret our behaviour – usually to our disadvantage. We are perhaps, unaware of the 'sharpness' in our tone of voice; in seminars we may not realise that our seemingly innocuous question is interpreted by the tutor as being unduly critical. "Why are you looking so miserable?" someone might say, when we are perfectly happy – just deep in thought. Sitting in a chair, tilted back, hands behind our head, may give the appearance of being 'laid back', when we are actually contemplating our next move. *The essential message running throughout these brief examples is simply that we are in much less control of the image that we project than we might think.* If we like the other person, we think that we demonstrate that in what we say and do; if we don't, we believe that we can conceal our feelings. We are probably wrong on both counts.

We tend to pay more attention to *what* we say than *the way we say it* and the accompanying body language. This is unfortunate, since psychologists believe that around 90% of our face-to-face communication is non-verbal. Additionally, it is our body language that is more likely to reveal our true feelings and attitudes. Unless we are aware of these points, we are likely to convey the wrong impression, and as mentioned previously, that first impression we have created will be difficult to rectify later.

The term body language includes eye contact, facial expressions, gestures and body movements, posture and stance, body contact, and appearance and physique. An exhaustive discussion of these points is outside the scope of this book, but a brief summary may serve to give the sports coach an appreciation as to how his best efforts may well be undermined if he ignores the potentially strong impact that body language can make[2].

Eye contact is the most powerful means of communication that we possess. Why that should be is not at all clear. Researchers have advanced a number of reasons for this, one being that we learn the significance of eye contact in childhood. We learn that certain kinds of 'look' from others – teachers, parents, and friends – indicate whether they like or dislike us. In the process of growing up, we also absorb many subtle 'rules' of eye contact and some of these will be specific to our Western culture, others not. Children are taught not to stare at people. As adults, we do not look at each other all the time when we are talking, taking care to ration our glances to a suitably brief length. The purpose of this is primarily to check that the other person understands what we are saying.

There are of course, exceptions. People having intensely personal conversations will hold each other's gaze for longer. 'Eye-balling' another person is considered to be aggressive, whilst too little eye contact conveys an impression of 'shiftiness', or shyness at the very least. Looking around a room whilst listening to someone will give the appearance of boredom. Lowering one's gaze will be interpreted as conceding a point – submission, in other words.

The next time you are in a public place, note the eye movements of those around you. You will be surprised at the variety of conversational implications that you can draw from a short observation.

So what is the significance of this for the coach? The purpose is simply to illustrate that it is important that we get our body language in line with our intentions. Further, we believe that our control over our body language, and its effect on others, is much higher than is actually the case. Thus, if we are sympathetic to the other person, we believe that this will show in our behaviour; if we are not sympathetic, we believe that we can conceal this. Because our non-verbal behaviour is more powerful than what we actually say, and if we are saying one thing, but our body language says something else, then it is the 'something else' that will be interpreted as the real message by others. I am sure I am not the only one who has noticed that President Clinton always has a smile – or a vestige of a smile - on his face, even when he is saying something serious. At the height of the Monica Lewinsky affair, when his political career was on the line, he still had that fleeting hint of a smile that made it appear as if it was all, in reality, a game. Similarly, when he talked about conflict in the Middle East, Bosnia or Kosovo, genocide, or the need for 'humanitarian aid', he still seemed to be smiling. Jerome Burne had this to say about smiling[3]: "There are 18 different sorts of smile but only one is genuine. Called the Duchenne smile, it needs two sets of muscles – one around the mouth called the zygomatic and the other around the eyes called the orbicularis . What makes it special is that while you can consciously control the mouth muscles, the orbicularis only responds to genuine emotion. Good cheat detectors also watch the left side of the face. A genuine emotion usually affects both sides of the face equally, but when the feelings are phoney there tends to be more activity on the left."

Not only are our eyes a powerful element in our body language but also of our total facial expression. It is through our facial expressions that we can convey our attitudes to others, not only of liking or disliking, but also of superiority, equality, and inferiority. Others are very sensitive to our attitudes of superiority and inferiority and if we fail to get it right it will be difficult to create the right impression subsequently. At the time of writing the Dutch manager of Newcastle United, Ruud Gullit, was being strongly criticised in some sections of the press for his alleged aloofness. Whether this aloofness is real or simply an impression that others have, is beside the point. If others believe that he is aloof on account of his non-verbal behavior then *that is the reality.*

---

Newcastle's captain, Alan Shearer, is said to be surprised if he gets so much as a "Hello" in the morning from his manager. The Daily Mail sports reporter said at the start of the 1999 season, that Gullit "is a man cursed with an ability to make people feel, deliberately or otherwise, as if he is quite unaware of their presence, let alone their feelings". He goes on to say, "How an evidently talented coach can miss the vital connection between good relations on the training ground and loyalty on the pitch is one of world football's greatest mysteries." When Gullit was manager of Chelsea, it has been reported that he seldom stayed around after training to eat in the players' canteen, and when he did, he usually sat apart from the others, dining on his own.

---

Can it be that Ruud Gullit is unaware of the negative impact his manner has on others? I believe it is quite possible. As stated earlier, our visible behaviour can be quite at odds with our true feelings.

Our postures are also strong indicators of attitude. When we lean forward whilst talking we create an impression of enthusiasm. When we sit upright in a chair, we tend to convey the impression of confidence and even authority. Slouching in a chair conveys slackness. When we are walking it is evident that those who walk with an upright stance, looking ahead and with shoulders back, will project a positive and self-confident image. Some researchers and writers on the subject of body language believe that many inferences can be drawn about our state of mind simply though our posture, and that this can give useful clues as to what the most productive approach is likely to be.

Whilst sitting opposite someone may be appropriate for a formal meeting, it is often more appropriate *not* to sit behind a desk if the subject matter is more personal. Experienced interviewers usually position a seat so they are not directly opposite the other person, because it is less likely to create defensive attitudes, and more likely to encourage honest exchanges. It is particularly appropriate when giving advice.

So you need to be alert to your body language as well as to the substance of what you are saying, and this is particularly true if you feel strongly about an issue. The chances are that unless you make a *conscious* effort to behave otherwise, your feelings will show clearly through your body language. Thus, when the coach is talking to his players, he needs to be sure that he is not sending the wrong signals through inappropriate body language. What he says should match his facial expression and gestures, otherwise the content may not be believed.

As mentioned earlier, creating a positive impression on other people is, in fact to produce a *performance*. Whether we like it or not all our interactions with others are, in effect, performances. As such they can create positive or negative attitudes in the mind of your players. If you feel that controlling your non-verbal behaviour is deceitful and something you have no wish to do, then you just need to be mindful that you are in danger of being misunderstood. Behaving naturally, can therefore work against your interests, whilst projecting *appropriate* body language will help to reinforce your message.

## Self image

One of the most influential factors in what is known as impression management, is our self-image. We referred to this earlier but now we need to look at it in more detail.

In trying to explain self-image or self-concept, psychologists have usually referred to the 'I' and the 'Me'. The 'I' is that part of the self that makes decisions and reacts to circumstances. The 'Me' is that part of the self that absorbs other people's reactions to us. Consider, as an example, "I am driving this car," (an 'I' statement), but "The people at work seem to like me," (a 'me' statement). We have 'internalised' these perceived attitudes of others and much of this internalisation takes place during childhood and our formative years.

There seems to be, therefore, two separate elements to our self-concept – the 'I' being a sense of ourselves as unique individuals, and the 'Me' being a coalescence of the attitudes of others towards us. The effect of these two elements provides us with our 'self-image' – who we think we are.

We convey this self-image in our contact with other people. If for example, we have been consistently thought by others to be stupid, it is likely that we will come to believe it. If others have consistently regarded us as determined and focused on objectives, it is likely that we may think of ourselves as ambitious and successful. As previously stated, much of this internalisation of social rules takes place in our formative years, and highlights the importance of the cricket coach (as well as teacher and parents, of course) in the development of the young cricketer.

If you were to write down a list of adjectives to describe yourself you will most probably use a mixture of physical description and then less concrete characteristics. The following is an example:

*Above average height, sturdy build, brown hair, wears spectacles, slightly round-shouldered, clean shaven, tense, enthusiastic for new projects/ideas, not a good finisher, ambitious, emotionally stable.*

Some of these words convey an impression of what we may believe about ourselves – our strengths and our weaknesses – and they will almost certainly therefore, influence our behaviour and our beliefs as to how others might behave towards us. Negative self-assessments will result in low self-esteem. (See Chapter 9 for a full explanation.) If we behave as if our opinions and actions are worthless, then we are likely to be treated in this way by others. Conversely, an over-estimation of our abilities can be equally damaging. The problem for most of us however, is that our self-esteem is likely to be lower rather than higher. It is a strange fact that we have a tendency to focus on the negative for much of the time, failing to give ourselves credit for our successes, and punishing ourselves for our failures. Certainly within our Western culture most of us are taught from an early age not to boast, and to be modest in our claims for achievement. The result is that not only are most of us modest, but that we fail to give ourselves credit for much that we do which is right.

This point is amply illustrated by research undertaken some years ago at UCLA – the University of California at Los Angeles – on the level of self-esteem in new undergraduates. Entrance to the university is demanding: only the very brightest make it. New undergraduates were asked to list on a sheet of paper words that were descriptive of themselves - negative words in the left-hand column and positive words in the right-hand column. Most undergraduates had an average ratio of about 6 negative words to 1 positive word, yet these were some of the most able young people in the country.

The image we project may be unbalanced or biased in some way and we may not be aware that the way in which we project ourselves shapes the impressions that others gain of us. The behaviour that we display outwardly impacts on how we feel inwardly. If you start to behave in a confident manner, by taking deep breaths, lowering the tone of your voice, and speaking very deliberately, you will start to feel more confident and of course, this will be conveyed to others. If you act as if you are angry, thereby simulating anger, you will very quickly actually *feel angry*. It is therefore by controlling our behaviour that we can project the desired image, and this will be easier than trying to control our thoughts.

We need to practice this if it is to change our self-esteem in a positive way. It will not work satisfactorily simply by using it on the odd occasion when you happen to remember it. If we work at it, it can improve our self-esteem, our self-concept, and thereby influence the impression we can create with others.

Finally, we need to deal with assertiveness since this is an important element in the way we present to others, and is also directly related to our self-esteem – or lack of it.

What is assertiveness? Is it the same as aggressiveness? Certainly not! Assertiveness is primarily about standing up for our rights, yet recognising that other people have rights too. It is the quality of being able to steer a middle course between being non-assertive, which may result in our rights being brushed aside by others, and being aggressive, in which you stand up for your own rights at the expense of those of other people.

In practice, most of us veer from being assertive in some situations, and being non-assertive in other situations. We determine which course to take depending on the circumstances, and perhaps the personalities involved – in short we read the situation before we decide to adopt a particular type of behaviour.

The following are situations that might require an assertive manner:

- Asking someone not to park in your reserved car parking space.

- Asking for time off.
- Asking someone to switch off a mobile telephone whilst in your meeting.
- Returning a purchase to a shop.
- Telling the waiter that your steak was not cooked to your liking.
- Explaining to your boss that an assignment will not be completed on time.
- Telling a senior player that he must be prompt for future net practices.

You will see from the above that much might depend on the circumstances of the situation. Whether someone is a boss or a subordinate, whether you are simply asking someone to obey rules, whether the other person is known to you or not – all these factors might influence your approach.

Some writers have observed that our behaviour is likely to vary dependent on whether we are asking for something for ourselves, or whether on behalf of another. For instance, disciplining a subordinate when necessary is an integral part of a management job – you have the stripes to impose it and you will be expected to do so by your boss – whereas asking for a pay rise is a more personal matter.

The alternatives to acting assertively bring their own disadvantages. The consistently unassertive person is likely to be ignored when it matters most that he should not be. The consistently aggressive person is likely to leave a trail of human relations problems behind him. Some people indeed can veer between these two extremes and this might occur with someone who is normally unassertive. There then comes a point at which they see their behaviour in perspective and decide that they need to be assertive. 'Thus far and no further,' might describe their thinking. Others however, might be puzzled as to why someone they knew to be unassertive suddenly appears to be the opposite. Conversely, but less frequently, those who often behave assertively might gain insight into their behaviour and overcompensate by being too submissive.

When a number of cricket coaches undertook a personality assessment, one of the most significant aspects of their profiles was their relatively low level of assertiveness. It can be argued that this might have its advantages. Highly assertive people will advance their opinions frequently and are not usually good listeners, but arguably the coach *does* need to be a good listener, and it seems that the *less* assertive might therefore strike a better balance between listening and acting assertively.

# CHECK LIST FOR PRESENTING YOURSELF

❖ According to Goffman, each meeting with another person is a 'performance' – whether we are aware of it or not.

❖ We reveal much of our true feelings and attitudes *unconsciously* through our body language. Coaches need to ensure that their body language matches their intentions.

❖ Our self- image is central to the manner in which we interact with others.

❖ Our self-image is formed early in life and our self-esteem will be low if we make unrealistically negative assessments of ourselves.

❖ A negative self-image will almost certainly be inaccurate. We need to think positively about ourselves and be aware that our *own behaviour* has an affect on us. This needs to be practised frequently for it to have an affect on our self-concept or self-image.

❖ We need to be assertive when it is appropriate. Assertiveness means standing up for your rights in a non-combative manner. Aggressiveness is standing up for your rights at the expense of someone else's and doing so in a belligerent manner.

# 3    Motivation

*To Britain they came from the land of the South*
*As strangers for honour and glory,*
*And now as true heroes intrepid and bold*
*Will their names be recorded in glory.*

*For not with the sword did they covet renown,*
*The battle they fought was at cricket,*
*In lieu of grim weapons of warfare they strove*
*With the bat and the ball at the wicket.*

Anon

"A coach must be able to motivate his players." Of course. We all know that. As mentioned earlier, many sports coaching books identify the need for the coach to be a motivator without giving the slightest indication as to how this might be achieved. Apparently one is just supposed to know these things!

Few subjects have received as much attention from psychologists as that of motivation. As an aspect of the management of others, that is easy to understand. Treating people well, and helping them to feel good about themselves would seem to be an obvious requirement. How you do this, and sustain it over a long period is quite another matter. For this we need to have a grasp of human behaviour, and be able to devise ways to motivate players in the short and the long term.

Psychologists have spent many years - and some their whole lives - in studying motivation and its affects. It seems surprising therefore, that we know so little about it. There are indeed many theories that have considerable appeal ranging from B. F. Skinner's conditioning theories, to Abraham Maslow's hierarchy of needs, Hertzberg's 'hygiene' factors, and McGregor's Theory X and Theory Y, and we shall discuss some of these topics in this chapter. But the cricket coach who looks for a 'formula' likely to work under all conditions is going to be disappointed. There may be an approach that works well in a given situation but nothing that works well in *all* situations, and further, although psychology is undoubtedly a science, it is not an *exact* science.

The role of both captain and coach are pivotal to the motivation of a cricket team, but here we will concentrate on that of the coach.

At least one writer[1] has advanced the idea that the personality of the coach might very well be sports specific, and of course his personality will determine how he motivates his team. It is also suggested that frequently a 'team personality' develops as a result of the interaction between the personalities of the coach and those of the team. If a coach is seen to be hard working, reliable, outgoing and confident, players may well copy that model. If the coach is seen to be lax, withdrawn, and perhaps lacking in confidence, then the players may reflect that also. What *does* appear to have some superficial validity is that certain sports seem to attract particular types of personality. An authoritarian coach is more likely to be drawn to football than to cricket, to ice hockey* rather than tennis. The more relaxed and sociable coach is not usually found in boxing, or, perhaps, rugby, but may be found in golf or cricket. It may well be that a particular type of personality, suited to a specific sport, may be more successful than another in motivating his players. However, the possibility of changing one's personality in any significant manner is unlikely. Some aspects of personality may be modified, but radical changes are almost always the result of dramatic events in one's life. The prudent cricket coach will spend much time in determining how to motivate individual players. Well-motivated individuals are more likely to lead to team success, although this is by no means a foregone conclusion. (See Chapter 12, Teamwork.)

First, how do we know that there is a need to improve motivation? Put another way, can we recognise low morale when we see it? Readers who have experience of visiting a variety of organisations, factories and offices, will tell you that they can sense when morale is low. There is a culture of blame and apathy that is conveyed in a myriad of ways. When morale is high and people are well motivated there is a buzz, and the visitor will gain the impression that everyone knows his job and is keen to do it. Where morale is low, discontent may show itself in such things as a lack of co-operation, a reluctance to do anything outside normal duties, not reaching agreed standards, and complaining about minor things.

---

* The Great Britain ice hockey coach, Peter Woods, backed his side's aggressive style to carry them through the 1999 World Championship qualifying match against Latvia. He said, "Latvia play pretty hockey, and we play not so pretty hockey, so I'm sure it will be interesting."

Players who display some of these characteristics are likely to be demotivated and their behaviour should give you clues as to how they are being managed. They are likely to make negative remarks about the team or the club as a whole. The problem is that those who regularly and frequently make negative remarks spread dissatisfaction. They become toxic people and thus poison those around them. Typically negative comments that might indicate low morale are:

*"We've tried this before and it didn't work."*

Maybe, but things *do* change – people, conditions, thinking, and situations. The inventor of WD40 tried to invent a water-displacing agent 39 times before he found the 40th attempt to be successful.

*"We never play well against this side."*

To which the reply should be "And you're never likely to with that sort of attitude!"

*"Nobody seems to tell me anything."*

But does he ever make an attempt to find out? We all have a part to play in communication – we need to be both receivers *and* transmitters.

*"Who cares? We're almost bottom of the league."*

And likely to stay that way with that sort of thinking.

No doubt the reader could add many more negative comments from his own experiences. These negative remarks are repeated and even those who started with high morale may become demotivated. The poison spreads.

When considering success in sport, most people think first of skill and then of motivation. Certainly one is an easier concept to grasp than the other. We can't observe motivation: we can only see the behaviour that results from high or low motivation. It is usually motivation that is considered to make the difference between winning and losing. If two cricketing sides are about equal in talent, then it is motivation that might determine the winning side. (The way in which sports coaches refer to the motivation of their teams is a source of constant amusement. The Australian rugby coach, speaking after his team beat France in the 1999 World Cup, provides an example.

"There was no way we were going into that game without knowing that we were playing for Australia". So football managers do not have a monopoly on the obvious. Well, perhaps most coaches faced with a microphone or a reporter's notebook might respond in the same way.)

Coaches always talk about the importance of motivation and they are right to do so. The findings of experimental psychologists support this view. As long ago as 1954, two psychologists[2] said, "Both ability and motivation are factors in performance and if either of them is entirely lacking the performance does not occur. Ability is like a machine which cannot do its work unless the power is supplied."

It is all too easy to blame poor performance on the lack of motivation, but there may be other reasons for this which need to be explored. (See Chapter Four, Attribution.) Lack of ability and insufficient training are two possibilities. Poor management may be another. Poor management? Yes, because that may lead to a lack of respect for control, such that players may do what they are told, but without conviction and enthusiasm. Domestic problems might also be a contributory factor.

So having found that there is a degree of low morale amongst a side or that motivation seems to be lacking amongst some of the players, what can the coach do about it? Before we attempt to answer this question, we need to understand the nature of motivation.

Motivation can be of two types – intrinsic and extrinsic. When the reward for the activity lies within itself, the motivation is said to be intrinsic. When the reward takes the form of money, that is, something lying outside itself, then motivation is said to be extrinsic, because the activity is primarily a means to an end. Rewards are more often seen as extrinsic - certainly this is true in many industrial and commercial organisations, perhaps because extrinsic rewards are easier to put into effect. Awarding or withholding a bonus or a pay rise is straightforward. Intrinsic rewards capitalise on one's pride and satisfaction in a job, and its power is often overlooked. Where an organisation has a group of employees who are professionally dedicated, keen to do their very best - then the intrinsic reward is likely to be a powerful motivator. Clearly though, some people are more attracted to extrinsic rewards. Maslow's theory states that extrinsic factors are likely to be important at an early stage, but when they have been achieved, intrinsic rewards are valued more highly. Putting it crudely, people first want money (and by implication, food, shelter and their basic needs provided for), and then they want opportunity for personal growth, followed by respectability (honour, awards, accolades, etc.)

There is one other point to make before we leave intrinsic and extrinsic rewards. A cricketer who plays for an external reason is playing for extrinsic motivation and therefore he is motivated partly by the prospect of reward. But what will happen to the cricketer's motivation if the reward is withdrawn? Certainly in the USA, research into attribution theory has found that withdrawal of external rewards to young athletes has damaged the intrinsic motivation to compete.

Other research seems to indicate that extrinsic rewards can either add or detract from intrinsic motivation. What happens is quite interesting. It seems that the locus of control can shift from an internal to an external source. Siedentopp and Ramey quote the following story:[3]

---

An elderly man was disturbed by very noisy children who consistently played near his home. He repeatedly asked them to play elsewhere, but to no avail. He tried several ideas, all of which failed. He then decided to entice them with money.

He offered them 20 cents each if they would come the following day and play in the same area, which they did. The following day, he offered them 15 cents to play there again. A few days later, he followed that up by offering them 10 cents and subsequently, 5 cents a day to play in the same area on successive days. At that point, the boys decided not to return because it wasn't worth it for just 5 cents. They went to play elsewhere!

The point here is that they had grown to believe that they were playing there for the money, and not for the fun of it and their locus of control had moved from an internal one to an external one.

Relating this to the wages of today's professional footballers, one wonders if any of them might be playing for the intrinsic reward of enjoying the game.

---

Douglas McGregor advanced his Theory X and Theory Y of motivational styles in 1960[4]. Broadly, this posited that Theory X style of management assumes that workers (players) need direction, that they can't take responsibility, that they are immature, dislike work, and are basically lazy. The Theory Y style of management assumes that the average person does not dislike work, that he can exercise self-direction and control if he is committed to objectives, that the potential of individuals is only partly realised, and that imagination is not the preserve of management, but is distributed fairly evenly throughout the population. Whilst he admitted that these two theories were not perfect, the two underlying assumptions are: that under a Theory X style of management, failure is blamed on the people being managed (the players), and that under Theory Y, failure is blamed on the management (the coach and the captain.) In other words, under Theory Y, management had failed to motivate people satisfactorily. (See Chapter 12, Leadership.)

Success and failure, the outcomes of motivation, cannot be seen in completely objective terms and it is important to take into account the sportsman's expectation, or aspiration, or both. Aspiration might be described as the condition that the sportsman hopes for, and under which he will be motivated to achieve ideal goals. Level of expectation refers to the pursuit of realistic goals. We can express these as two simple statements:

*The level of aspiration - actual performance = goal discrepancy,*
*The level of expectation - performance = attainment discrepancy.*


How much discrepancy will the individual cricketer tolerate? If his level of expectation is realistic, but his performance falls short of this, then he can be said to have failed. But if he has allowed a slightly more generous margin, (his expectations are lower), then that same performance might be regarded as being successful. This leads to the conclusion that success and failure can only be defined in terms of the individual's actual achievement and his aspirations, and are not therefore absolutes. This is *not* woolly thinking or simply playing with words! It is a fact.

Some psychologists believe that achievement motivation can be extended from the individual performance to that of groups. The assumption is that a team that is highly motivated is likely to select a moderately challenging goal, but a team that is highly motivated to *avoid failure*, is likely to choose goals where the odds are weighted heavily in their favour. Therefore there needs to be a compromise.

The 'self-fulfilling prophecy' is relevant here. If a team has failed often in the past, perhaps against a certain side, it may believe it will fail again. This is one reason why success should not be seen solely in the absolute terms of win or lose. If a team has failed frequently, individual players will feel inadequate, and membership of the team may become less important. If membership of the team originally had a high motivational factor, it follows that motivation will decrease, performance will deteriorate, and thus the 'self-fulfilling prophecy' will have been proved to be correct once again. "I've failed before, and I'll fail this time." So you do. "We never beat this side away from home." So you don't. The key point here is that if the individual, or the team, had selected a less ambitious target, it might have had a greater chance of succeeding. All very well, the coach might say, but the target is set by others - the supporters, the media, and the committee. And this is certainly a difficulty, preventing the team from setting more realistic objectives, and almost ensuring their failure.

Allowing the team and the individual to set their own targets therefore has clear advantages, if this can be done. Frank Dick, the former national coach who transformed Great Britain's athletic performances in the 70s and 80s, maintains that his athletes usually set themselves tougher objectives in training than he did[5]. Dick has explained elsewhere[6] his belief that good coaching methods should concentrate on building on people's strengths, the things they are good at. Most coaching and development, he says, both in sport and in industry, seems to focus on what people do badly, in the hope that they will eventually do it better. It is certainly true that people enjoy doing what they do best, and if coaches really want to build self-esteem and confidence, two elements of high performance, then they would do well to pay at least as much attention to what the player does well.

Frank Dick says that in the early stages of his relationship with an athlete, he used an authoritarian style of management. As the athlete progressed, and more of his motivation came from within, he needed less of the coach's authoritarian approach and more personal encouragement. * He used this approach with such athletes as Seb Coe, Daly Thompson, Steve Cram and Steve Ovett, and Sally Gunnell and Linford Christie.

It is quite likely that some cricketers may focus more on their mistakes than on success. One cricketer told me that in a particular match, he had difficulty in focusing on the number of runs needed. He was much more concerned to avoid making mistakes. He was

---

* See Chapter 12, Leadership for detail of research on successful coaching styles.

therefore focusing not on the need to succeed, but on his fear of putting in a poor performance. On that point, Paul Farbrace, a national coach with the ECB, had this to say:

*"I frequently see cricketers batting with completely the wrong attitude. They're scared of making a mistake and instead of playing with natural flair, which most love to do, they fiddle about and play negatively."*

From this we can deduce that the avoidance of failure is at least as powerful as the motivation to win. Translating this to the succession of average or poor performances by some members of the England cricket team in recent years, could it be that the motivation to play outstandingly, has been submerged by the fear of putting in an inferior performance, with the result that some cricketers have been satisfied with an average performance?

Another factor that also affects our motivation is conflict. This is present in one form or another in almost everything we do. If we decide to take a certain course of action, there will be advantages and disadvantages that flow from that action. Consider the following:

A young cricketer has been offered the chance of a good job at weekends for which the pay is good. He will be required to work both Saturday and Sunday. The school's cricket coach has told him that he has some talent and he is encouraged to play for the local team. If he opts for the part time job, and gives up his chance of playing cricket, he will have the benefits of gaining some much-needed cash and some useful work experience. The downside will be that he will have lost the chance to develop his cricketing skills, the admiration of his friends and family perhaps, and all the attention that a good sportsman is likely to attract in the community. If he opts for the chance to play cricket he will have the respect, camaraderie, and the knowledge that he is nurturing a talent. Either way there are disadvantages. Not all the factors will carry equal weight of course, but what he decides to do will be the result of the difference between these two driving forces. Either way, his motivation may be influenced by his realisation of what he has forsaken – the benefits of a job or the benefits of playing cricket.

Among the many psychologists who have studied motivation, the best known are Abraham Maslow (1908 – 1970) and Frederick Hertzberg (1923 -  ).

Maslow believed that we have a succession of needs commencing with a basic need for survival, security, social interaction, self-esteem, and the fulfilment of potential – sometimes called 'self-actualisation'. When each need is satisfied, the next one becomes important. As mentioned earlier, rewards are described as being either extrinsic or intrinsic. Intrinsic rewards – recognition, responsibility, and achievement - contribute to job satisfaction. If we are allowed more control over our jobs, if our opinions are sought, if we are given sincere praise, then job satisfaction increases. The extrinsic factors – pay, working conditions, and in fact all the more tangible elements of reward, Hertzberg called 'hygiene' factors. These are not long term motivators, but are more likely to be related to job dissatisfaction. This is easily verified through our own experience. If we receive an increase in pay, we are pleased for a few weeks at most, but eventually, we might think, "I've only got it because I'm worth it," or "they're simply paying me the market rate." The motivational effect is short-lived. Intrinsic rewards are more permanent and therefore of more interest to the cricket coach.

So money *per se* is not a strong motivator in the longer term. If newspaper reports are to be believed, there are many footballers earning tens of thousands of pounds a week who have low morale, are unsettled, and are unsettling their team-mates. Once our basic needs for survival are met, and we seek a higher social status, an expensive car or a grander house might fulfil that need, although for some people more than others. Even an important-sounding job title may be sufficient for some.

The higher levels of Maslow's motivational theory, that of realising personal ambitions, will be the most effective tool for the coach. The majority of people want to do better, to set themselves objectives and to realise them. Certainly the professional cricketer is in an exceptionally privileged position compared to most of the working population. He is already doing something he is good at and which is pleasurable. So that particular need is being satisfied. The next need will be to do better – achieving a place in the first team, playing regularly for one's county, even becoming a Test player. The pursuit of such objectives will become a continuous process.

Although the higher needs are influential, they will not come into play until the lower ones are met. Thus, if an individual seeks higher social status and this need is frustrated, he is likely to attach greater importance to a lower one – money for example. *A potential source of satisfaction becomes more important the less it is satisfied. This is the engine that drives ambition.*

The process of motivating players to perform better requires the following prerequisites:

1) identifying the reasons for poor performance,
2) eliminating negative attitudes,
3) understanding personal needs.

The reasons for poor performance are examined in the next chapter, but briefly, they can be attributed to either:

**Lack of training.**   Is training made enjoyable, or has it become something of a chore, holding little or no appeal?  Remember that people usually operate best when there is an element of fun in the activity.  The ECB Cricket Coaches' Manual provides plenty of examples to make cricket practice enjoyable.

**Lack of ability.**   Has the player got the necessary skill base?  He does not need the potential of a Test player, but has he acquired – or can he acquire - basic technical skills that will improve performance at an appropriate level?

**Poor coaching.**   If previously, players have been badly coached, then they may have lost the respect that is vital.  It is usually difficult to change people's attitude and perception if they have had bad experiences of this sort and it will take time.

The best antidote to negative attitudes is for the coach to provide a continuous and believable example of positive attitudes. This is not to imply unrealistic and 'pie in the sky' attitudes.  He can maintain a positive outlook by being enthusiastic about the tasks to be tackled; by letting others know that he is committed to these objectives; listening to what they have to say; encouraging individual members of the team.  He needs to keep a clear focus on positive things – the good things that people do – rather than concentrating on the negative – the things that people may do less well.  If the coach is clear about his own values and objectives, this is likely to enthuse others, because whether he is aware of it or not, he will be communicating those values to others. Enthusiasm is infectious.  Capitalise on that fact. The consequence will be that people are more highly motivated.

The third factor, that of understanding personal needs requires the cricket coach to remember that different things motivate different people, because as stated earlier, players will be at different stages in their hierarchy of needs. Some will be motivated by money, others by improved status. Most people are responsive to praise, providing it is sincere and not used lavishly. The coach needs to reward the behaviour he wishes to encourage and to punish (withhold rewards) for behaviour he wishes to discourage. Some people will respond favourably by being given more responsibility, and others seek some degree of security. A common mistake is to believe that the same things that motivate us as individuals also motivate others.

That might work at the individual level, but how do you motivate a whole team? That can only be achieved through the influence of each team member who, if well motivated, will produce the glue that is likely to encourage cohesiveness in a team and thus generate a higher level of morale and motivation. The knowledge that you are playing with others who are not only competent but are playing well is itself a motivator, and of course, nothing succeeds like success.

---

Paul Johnson, senior player with Nottinghamshire County Cricket Club, recalls the motivation of the team in the early 1980s. "I joined Notts in 1981. There was a very talented team of 8 internationals. The captain was Clive Rice and Ken Taylor the manager. Notts won the championship in 1981. They had 9 match winners in the side, and this in itself, seemed to provide the motivation as well as the team spirit. There was a massive belief in each person's ability."

---

The coach will be making advances if he can first, determine whether there is a lack of motivation, then diagnose possible reasons as to why this might be, and then try to identify the causes of poor performance.

An important constituent of motivation is that of goal setting. Like all sportsmen, cricketers need strategies to keep going in the face of setbacks – during the off season, and when dropped from the team for example. Goal setting is a basic aspect of a player's development. It is a means of identifying the stages through which the player will need to pass in order to accomplish his main objective. The goal may be to learn or improve an existing technique, or to reach a specific standard. Goal setting is essential to improved performance. Motivation on its own is merely an empty concept; setting realistic goals provides the motivation a player needs if he is to be successful. The very act of determining goals is in itself, motivational. A coach cannot motivate a player in a vacuum. However the setting of suitable goals does need some thought if they are to be of value. They need to be S – M – A – R –T. SMART is an acronym for:

**S**pecific
**M**easurable
**A**ttainable
**R**ealistic
**T**ime-based

These are the building blocks to improved performance.

Let's look at each of these in more detail.

*A goal needs to be specific*, or how else can the player be sure he has attained it?    Before a goal is set, the coach and the player need to discuss what might be the most relevant goal to attain.   To do this, the coach needs to determine what the player has done so far in order to achieve it, and how close he has come to achieving it.   Current levels of performance need to be agreed and the goal needs to be placed in this context.    A goal cannot be something as vague as being a 'regular member of the team', or 'playing in the 1st XI.' These are simply ideas – good ideas – but *only* ideas, not goals. The problem is that these 'outcomes' do not provide a specific course of action to get there.

As far as possible it needs to be *measurable*. "If it exists in any quantity at all, it can be measured."  A little overstated perhaps, but the underlying reasoning is sound.

*Attainability* is an obvious element.   A goal should not be so difficult that the prospect of achieving it is remote.   That will do nothing for confidence or morale. Targets have to be realistic and if they are set too low, they will lack challenge and the player is unlikely to gain any real sense of satisfaction in achieving it.   As previously mentioned, Frank Dick, maintains that his athletes often set themselves tougher targets than he would have done. Tennis star Tim Henman at the end of what was a poor season for him, said, *"I was so disappointed with the way the year finished that I didn't really think I deserved a break.  I went back on court immediately and started working on my game.  I've been working straight through since."*

Finally, the player will need to work towards his target within a *time frame*, otherwise things will begin to drift and the original motivation may fall off.

When done correctly, goal setting will provide a focus for the player's efforts. It has been shown to be a positive influence on performance because it directs action to the relevant area; it provides a focus for effort, and the effort can be expended over a period of time. The coach who sets tough but attainable goals will produce better players than the one who simply asks a player to 'do his best'. Goals need to be based on individual ability and performance.

Listen to Allan Donald, one of the world's fastest bowlers, speaking at the World Cricket Cup Coaches' Conference in 1999:

"Goal setting has played a big role in my career. I aim for 20 – 25 wickets in every Test series. Sometimes you wake up in the morning and you're not ready for this. Especially when the opposition is 320 – 2. But it's all about being professional. Go out there and do the job. There are going to be days when you feel you don't want to play the game – that comes with it. My motivation is setting myself goals, every time, I drive myself towards that 25 wickets or whatever it is. When you've taken a couple of wickets the night before, the next morning is a good motivation. I aim to get 5 wickets in a test match – it's as good as a batsman's hundred. It's very important to get through that first over."

How does this square with our criteria for goal setting? Very well, I think. It is specific, it is measurable, achievable (for someone with his bowling ability), realistic, and it is time-based.

So the coach can save valuable time by mapping out a specific course of action for improved performance. Frank Dick talks about the coach needing to 'dream, then plan, then view, and then review.' In my early days as a judo player I spent many hours practising. I had the dream – to be a better competitor – but did none of the other things that Dick recommends. Progress was slow because (with hindsight) my efforts had insufficient focus. Certainly there were spells of practising a specific throw, but usually for a short period, spasmodically, and not as part of an integrated approach. How much better it would have been if I had directed my attention to say, groundwork for several weeks at a time, mastering important holds in a variety of situations. I could have determined the strategies and skills likely to be needed in competition; that path would have led to greater success. Much of my effort was wasted because it lacked almost everything we have just referred to: my training goals were not specific, not measurable – and therefore not attainable, not very realistic, and certainly not time-based.

Focus, effort, persistence and the development of skills are all dimensions of motivation, and all can be the product of goal setting.

Goals should always be expressed in positive terms. Thus, "I hope to improve my bowling this season", is too vague to be regarded as a goal. It is not specific or measurable and therefore not realistic, although it might have been attainable if these two factors had been included in the statement. What is more likely to succeed as a goal is to say, "As a leg spin bowler I am going to work on run-up and delivery over the next four weeks, aiming for maximum spin and control of the ball."

Coaches should not expect individual performance to improve smoothly. It goes up in stages, as motivation waxes and wanes. We cannot be highly motivated for 100% of the time.

---

An interesting example of the importance of focus and motivation, lies in the recent career of tennis star Andre Agassi. He made a comeback by winning the French Open title, and then being runner-up at the men's singles final at Wimbledon. He said that, the failure of his 1997 marriage to Brooke Shields was a source of anguish and soul-searching but it was also the "catalyst for a return to the intensity of focus" that propelled him to victory in the French Open. Coming from two sets down, he demonstrated that his marriage break-up, far from hampering him, had the opposite affect. The worst moment of his career came in November 1997 in the Las Vegas Challenger tournament while top players were competing in Hanover. He was defeated in the final by an unknown German. "That was terrible," said Agassi, "I wasn't confused as to why I was going down the pan. I wasn't putting the same intensity and focus into my tennis. I got to the point where I was just embarrassed to be on court.   I couldn't compete on nearly the same level and had to make a decision in my heart and mind about what I had to do.   I knew I had more tennis in me.   I wanted to start over again and my mind was made up."

---

Six months later, Agassi's successes seem now to be routine.   In recent months he has won 3 grand slams out of four.   He said:

*"I was losing in the fourth round of the French Open, but then I decided I would refuse to lose by not hitting my shots.   I started playing incredibly aggressive tennis and turned the match around.   I realised I had had a great year in 1998 but I didn't execute in the biggest of matches.   That's when I really started letting my game fly and then I swore that I would always do that from there on in."*

So motivation goes up and down, perhaps matching successes and failures, but performance rises in steps.   After New Zealand's victory in the second Test at Lord's in 1999, their captain, Stephen Fleming, said that their victory had been targeted 18 months previously.

---

"Compared with England our history is quite young and we used the fact that we had never won here in 68 years as a motivating force.   There were some very emotional players in the dressing room afterwards," he said.   He believed that England might have underestimated his side at the start of the series.   "It was probably hard not to," he said, "because all I read in the newspapers is that we lack flair and flamboyancy and have no personalities."

So "negative publicity" can be a motivating force.   As Richard Hobson of The Times said during the third Test against New Zealand, "Mistakenly dismissed as underdogs, New Zealand have used all the negative publicity as a motivational tool.   The personalities within a squad fallaciously portrayed as being devoid of character have held their tongues, smiled knowingly to themselves, and played good cricket."

---

The final comment from Fleming came at the end of the fourth Test at The Oval which England lost by 83 runs thereby losing the series, and placing them bottom of the Wisden World championship rankings: "Our batting was not great through the series, but the bowlers put pressure on England by being aggressive. You could say we wanted it more, but I think confidence was the key. Hunger always comes from confidence."

# CHECK LIST FOR MOTIVATION

❖ Motivation is key to successful performance. Essentially, it is about helping players to feel good about themselves.

❖ The personality of the coach can be an important factor in motivating his team.

❖ Learn to recognise the indicators of low morale. Try to understand the reasons for this.

❖ Motivation can be intrinsic or extrinsic. Intrinsic factors are those that develop pride, self-esteem, and satisfaction. Extrinsic factors such as money, are short-term motivators.

❖ McGregor's Theory X assumes that people dislike work and responsibility and are basically lazy. Theory Y assumes the opposite – that when people are well motivated they will assume responsibility, commit to objectives, and wish to fulfil their potential.

❖ If a player's performance falls short of his realistic expectations, he can be said to have failed, but if he lowers his expectations, the same performance will have been successful. Winning and losing should not always be regarded as absolutes.

❖ Success and failure are subjective rather than absolute. Goals should be S-M-A-R-T – specific, measurable, attainable, realistic, and time-based.

❖ Reward the behaviour that you wish to encourage.

❖ A potential source of ambition becomes more important the less it is fulfilled. This drives ambition.

❖ Motivating players to perform better is a three-stage process: identify reasons for poor performance; eliminate negative attitudes by example; try to understand personal needs.

# 4    Attribution theory

*With dignity he made his way*
*Back to the dumb pavilion.*
*I must say his mien was proud, his gait firm and steady,*
*And as upon the scoring-board they stuck,*
*With callous haste, a large and hideous duck,*
*He said, in a high clear accent, "What putrid luck,*
*I wasn't ready."*

*With Dignity and Calm*
Anon

The batsman in this poem attributed his duck to 'putrid luck'. In fact he made two *attributions*, one to luck and the other to the fact that he was not ready. Attribution is the name given by psychologists to the reasons we attach to success or failure. *Attribution theory* is an important and useful concept for the cricket coach to grasp in the evaluation of his players' success or failure, and so we will deal with it in some detail. It describes one way of looking at motivation by examining the way in which players give reasons for their own behaviour. These reasons are called *causal interpretations* but first, let us look at another example of attribution.

During the warm-up games prior to the 1999 World Cricket Cup, Zimbabwe lost to Derbyshire. The Zimbabwe coach David Houghton, accused his team of playing 'schoolboy cricket'. Although Derbyshire were missing their front-line seamers, Dominic Cork and Kevin Dean, they still managed to win by five wickets. After the match Houghton said, "We just had a bad day. No-one was knocking the ball around for singles and it was almost schoolboy cricket." Let's consider those words - "We had a bad day."

## Internal and external attribution

Having a 'bad day ' could mean a number of things, some of them within the control of the players, and some not. If he meant that they were unlucky, for example in losing a vital wicket due to the unexpected bounce of the ball, this would have been outside the control of the Zimbabwe team, and might therefore be regarded as an acceptable reason for failure.    Such reasons – or attributions - for failure are said to be *external*. If Houghton had said that his team had not tried hard enough, then the attribution would be said to be *internal* because the amount of effort was within their control.    You will see from Fig. 2 that not only are attributions described as internal and external, but also as *stable* and *unstable*.    Effort and luck are unstable in the sense that both can vary. Ability is classed as internal, but also as stable, or at least relatively stable.  Ability can be improved upon, but is largely a matter of innate talent.  Certainly ability is not going to vary within the course of a game.

|  | INTERNAL | EXTERNAL |
|---|---|---|
| stable | Ability | Difficulty of task |
| unstable | Effort | Luck |

**Figure 2**
Weiner's classification scheme

Attribution theory is not new.  Fritz Heider first formulated it in 1944, and because it concentrates on concepts that people use in everyday life, it is sometimes described as a *common sense,* or *naïve, psychology.*

In 1958 Heider developed his theory further[1], and in more recent times Bernard Weiner who adapted the principles, firstly in regard to academic success and failure, and later to suit the needs of sport psychology[2] has built on them further.

From Fig. 2 it is clear that the process of attribution combines personal (internal) and environmental (external) factors. We can control the personal factors but not the environmental ones. Therefore, if a batsman fails, he might say that his failure was due to lack of effort on his part (*internal*) and that is something over which he has control.  Perhaps he needs to spend more time in the nets.  But he might also say that he was unlucky - perhaps the ball hit an uneven patch and fooled him.  That would be external attribution because he had no control over it.

## Protecting self-esteem

So what does this mean for the coach?  You will recall that in an earlier chapter we referred to self-esteem as being the core of our self-image. The strength of our self-esteem reflects our feelings of self-worth. It seems that we often produce attributions that serve to protect our self-esteem. Therefore, if a batsman fails he might attribute the cause to an external factor - the difficulty of the task or a bad umpiring decision - rather than to an internal factor such as his own lack of ability or lack of effort. In this way, his self-esteem will be protected.

Some sport psychology researchers have found that internal attributions are made more often when players are successful. So the success will be put down to ability, or to the effort that may have recently been expended. In this way the batsman will be protecting his self-esteem. But when an individual fails, this is much less likely to be ascribed to internal factors. It is much easier on the ego to say that the failure was due to an external factor such as bad luck, a poor umpiring decision, or anything else that was outside the batsman's control.

An outcome in the sense that we are using the word here, is the result of the combination of such factors as personality, intention, ability, and effort, and situational factors such as available options and the difficulty of the task. We can see therefore, that faced with the outcome, the cricketer will seek to explain the result to his own satisfaction.

## The evaluation of success and failure

Cricket coaches have to evaluate the performances of team members, and therefore they need to decide the extent to which players are responsible for their own performances. Is success or failure a matter of ability, or the lack of it? To what extent is effort a factor? And what about luck and the quality of the opposition? It is obvious that some factors are largely to do with us as individuals, and others are not. So where do we place the blame for success or failure? Attribution theory maintains that we need to assign causes to events in our lives, and thus make sense out of those events.

Let's refer back to the example of the Zimbabwe cricket team being beaten by Derbyshire. David Houghton's comment that his team had a 'bad day', is somewhat vague but admirably suits our purpose as an example.

He could mean any one of the following:

- *the team lacked concentration:* this would be an *internal* attribution because firstly it relates to the person, and secondly it is something over which the individual batsman has control - he could display more concentration at the wicket. It is also an *unstable* attribution because concentration can vary.

- *the team were unsuited to the Derbyshire wicket condition.* This is an *external* attribution since it is outside the control of the Zimbabwe batsmen. It is also *stable* because the wicket could be in the same condition if they have to play on it again.

- *the team may have come up against a side with more talent.* If Zimbabwe played the same team again, the opposition would still be difficult to beat if it were more talented. It is therefore *external* and *stable*.

- *there was a mix-up over the cricket gear and the travel arrangements.* Because they arrived late at the cricket ground, they had no time for their usual pre-match preparation, and their performance suffered. This would be *external* and *unstable* since the same thing is not likely to happen again.

The important thing is how the attribution can be classified within the dimensions shown in Fig. 2. If the coach saw the reason for failure as being internal and stable, there is little he can do about it other than to replace given players and thus have a more talented team. If he classifies the failure of his team as internal and unstable, then clearly there is something that can be done about it. They will have to develop their powers of concentration when at the wicket.

Matches against Zimbabwe seem to suit our purpose well, because another example of attribution was provided when England beat Zimbabwe by just one wicket in the winter tour of 1999 – 2000. With Zimbabwe at 131 all out, England were 120 for five with 10 overs left. Then England threw away four wickets for five runs inside four overs. Newspaper reports at the time commented not just on England's need to cope with stress, but also to avoid complacency, saying that there was a devil-may-care smugness about the middle order. Craig White had taken a career-best five for 21, and was comfortably in command of the England innings when he ended it with a flourish, caught by Goodwin. What attribution did Craig White make – caught whilst on 26? He said:

> *"We know we mucked up.   I thought we were home with*
> *just nine to win.   I was hoping to finish it with three*
> *boundaries, but I holed out to cover point.   When we lost a*
> *couple of quick wickets it put pressure on the bottom order.*
> *It shouldn't have happened.   Nobody doubts that the boys*
> *are tired, but it's no excuse.  If you have an England shirt on,*
> *you shouldn't need motivation."*

Clearly, it was internal and unstable.  So there must be hope…

## Locus of control

One psychologist[3] studied the extent to which people felt in control of their lives or not.   He called this the *locus of control*.  People who felt in control of their lives - that they could determine its course to a large extent - were described as having an internal locus of control, and those who felt that they were the victims of circumstances - luck, for example - were said to have an external locus of control.

One conclusion from his study was that those who had an internal locus of control were more mature, because they believed themselves to be in charge of the main events of their lives.   Transferring this to sport, those who identify the reasons for their success or failure as internal are likely to develop strong emotions such as pride or shame. Pride would follow a success that the batsman could genuinely attribute to his skill, or effort, or concentration - any characteristic that was particular to him.  Similarly failure might result in the belief that he had 'let the side down', and could result in him feeling ashamed. When success comes as a result of an external attribution, such as luck, then the batsmen's satisfaction will be far less, because he wants the success to come as a result of his own performance, not as a result of something over which he has no control.

An additional factor is that unstable and stable attributions are a reflection of past experiences.  If Midshires CCC has not beaten the League Champions Northshire CCC for the last three seasons, there will be an expectation that they will not beat them this time.  ("We never do.") This will be a stable attribution. If, to everyone's surprise they do beat them, then this will be attributed to luck.  In the England v Scotland Euro 2000 qualifying matches England, with a successful record behind them, were expected to win the 1st leg, which they did, 2 – 0 at Hampden Park.  Against all the odds, Scotland won the return match at Wembley, 1 - 0, and some accounts attributed this success to an un;table factor, luck. From England's point of view, because they had a successful record against Scotland over many years, (and were playing at home), they were expected to win. Since they didn't, they probably attributed this to an unstable factor, indicating that this factor might change next time. If they attributed their defeat to an internal and stable factor, it could mean that they felt they did not have the necessary skill, but their record against Scotland has proved otherwise.

## Errors of attribution

Whether players choose stable or unstable attributions for our results, is a critical issue for the coach, because it shows how players respond to failure, and also gives an indication about their maturity. If they believe the reasons to be stable, and they are correct, then as coaches, we can't change it. But fortunately, attributions are not always correct, and we need to understand why this is so.

When as players, we make an attribution about the outcome of our efforts, we may have a tendency to be lenient with ourselves. As mentioned earlier, this may be because we are mindful of our self-esteem and the effect that the admission of failure might have on it. If as a batsman, I have a successful innings, I am likely to attribute this to internal reasons i.e. something to do with me as a person. I might say that I have been working on my stroke play since the last season and this has paid off. This will be good for my self-esteem. However, my success could be due to poor bowling, an external attribution. An admission of this sort will do nothing for my self-esteem of course.

## Maturity and potential

The perceptive coach will now realise that whether his players choose internal or external attributions, and whether these are stable or unstable, says a lot about that player's potential as well as his maturity. Players who attribute their success to internal reasons are likely to have higher self-esteem and they are likely to be proud of their achievements. They are also likely to expect success, and the self-fulfilling prophecy, referred to in the last chapter, is likely to come into play. If they also attribute their failures to unstable factors, then they are in effect, saying that these factors can change and that they need not fail on the next occasion.

Those who are unsuccessful are likely to attribute their failure to stable factors and may therefore give up. ("I haven't got the ability".) The importance of this factor in coaching young players is obvious. *The coach needs to help the player to change his attributions.* If he can genuinely induce the player to think that success is within his control, then the player's expectation of success next time will be greater. If he attributes failure to unstable factors, he will believe that he might be successful on the next occasion.

## Interpersonal skills

We have said that attribution theory is applicable to the evaluation of success and failure, but it also affects our interpersonal skills, and it is well worthwhile for the coach to be alert to this fact.

Let us consider an example. Cricket coach James, knows that batsman Fred has said something that is untrue. His future attitude to Fred is likely to be affected by whether he thinks someone else has misinformed Fred, or whether he thinks Fred is lying. If he thinks Fred has been misinformed, he will attribute the untruth to *the situation.* If he thinks Fred is deliberately lying, he will attribute it to him *as a person.* He will regard it as a character defect and is likely to be sceptical about future statements.

## Controllability

During the 1970s attribution theory was researched extensively, and in 1979 Weiner added a third dimension to the two previously mentioned. This was *controllability.* He stated that some attributions are under the control of the player and some are not. Effort remains as the only one of Weiner's original four attributions that is controllable.

Locus of control and stability affect our feelings and expectations about our future performances, and likewise the controllability factor affects our behaviour. We reward and punish people according to our perception of their attributions that are controllable.

## Learned helplessness

In 1975 Carol Dweck evolved the theory of what she called 'learned helplessness'[4]. Her work was carried out with children, but the conclusions are valid for sport psychology and show that the attributions that players give for their failures can be changed.

The children that Dweck worked with were classed as helpless, and saw failure as the inevitable outcome of their efforts. In that sense, their attributions were stable. In her study, she gave half the children an easy task and therefore they succeeded. The other half were given some tasks in which they were successful and some in which they failed. Of the failures, Dweck specifically attributed the failure to a lack of effort (an unstable attribution which can therefore be changed.) This encouraged them to make more effort, and generally improved their performance because Dweck had been successful in changing their attribution from "I'm going to fail," to "I can do it if I try harder." She had changed the children's attribution of failure from stable to unstable. The 50% of the children who were given the easy tasks, and who all succeeded did not improve their performance and did not learn to cope effectively with failure.

As stated earlier then, it seems that the attributions for failure can be changed, and this conclusion has much significance for the cricket coach who can help players to be more successful by attributing that success to stable, internal, and controllable factors.

# CHECK LIST FOR ATTRIBUTION THEORY

❖ We tend to give reasons or attributions, for our successes and failures.

❖ These can be either internal, relating to ourselves and over which we have control, or external, relating to the environment and over which we have no control.

❖ A grasp of attribution theory is critical to the cricket coach if he is to understand his players better. He needs to see how they respond to success and to failure. It will also help him gauge their maturity.

❖ The causes for our successes and failures will either be stable or unstable. Unstable ones can be changed, stable ones cannot. The cricket coach needs to be mindful of this, encouraging players to attribute success to internal, stable factors.

❖ Because unstable attributions can be changed, the coach is in a position to influence players' attitude to failure and to help them achieve more success.

# 5    Arousal, stress and anxiety

*"Cricket was a manly game.  Manly masters spoke of
'the discipline of the hard ball'.  Schools preferred
manly games.  Games were only manly if it were possible
when playing them to be killed or drowned or, at the
very least, badly maimed.  Cricket could be splendidly
dangerous.  Tennis was not manly, and if a boy had
asked permission to spend the afternoon playing croquet
he would have been instantly punished for his 'general
attitude'."*

*The Crooked Bat*
Arthur Marshall

In this chapter we look at these terms – arousal, stress and anxiety -
and relate them to sport performance generally and cricket in particular.
Of these three words, stress in particular has become such a popular
topic in recent years that the reader might be forgiven for thinking
that unless he has suffered from it, he is not regarded as being
'committed', and therefore has not been working hard! Arousal,
stress, and anxiety are often used as if they are synonymous, but
psychologists have tried to draw distinctions between them.

## Arousal

We need to start, however with arousal. This word is often used
nowadays in a sexual context.  Here, we are using the word to describe
both physiological and psychological activity that is brought about by
a perceived threat. If we plotted levels of arousal as a continuum,
one end would signify the level of arousal in deep sleep – virtually
nothing - and the other end, the level of arousal during extreme
excitement. When we experience fear or anger a number of bodily
changes occur, and the purpose of these changes is to prepare the
body for action, (fight or flight). Typically, they might include:

- an increase in blood pressure and heart rate
- rapid breathing

- an increase in perspiration
- 'butterflies' in the stomach
- trembling

Less obviously, we might experience:

- an increase in blood-sugar level to provide more energy
- quicker blood clotting in case of wounds
- blood being diverted from the stomach to the brain and skeletal muscles

Additionally, endorphins are released from the brain into the blood stream, and these have the affect of acting as painkillers, producing the same effect as morphine. We have all experienced a cut or bruise without having the least idea of what caused it because something else demanded our whole attention at the time. Pupils may also dilate, allowing more light to penetrate the eye and thus sharpening eyesight. Hearing becomes more acute as the acoustic nerves are stimulated.

All these symptoms are the product of what is known as the autonomic nervous system – a set of physiological responses or changes, which occur without any conscious effort on our part. It would be reasonable to assume that these reactions are useful to the cricketer. The answer is Yes, up to a point.

Let's look at Figure 3, which illustrates the effect of arousal on performance. With little or no arousal, performance is at a very low level. As the physical and psychological effects of arousal develop, performance improves until it reaches a peak, after which it begins to drop off, until at its most extreme, the player would be unable to move freely. Of course the graph is a theoretical picture of what we believe actually happens, and in practice performance and arousal may not increase and decrease as smoothly as depicted.

This theory, known as the 'Inverted U' theory, was first proposed by Yerkes and Dodson[1], and has received fairly consistent support from sport psychologists. It also appeals to the layman since it offers a 'common sense' approach to the performance/arousal relationship. It has been criticised however, because although it shows the relationship, it does not *explain* it. Also, the smoothness of the curve may be OK as a theory, but in practice performance may fall off dramatically rather than gradually[2].

Two other factors relating to arousal are of interest. First, the level of arousal seems to be connected to the type of sport being

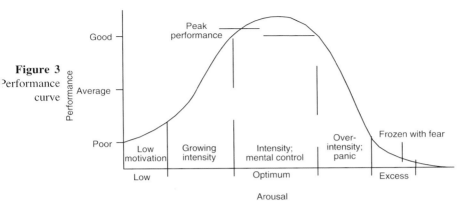

**Figure 3**
Performance
curve

played. Putting at golf and making a hard tackle at rugby would be at opposite ends on a scale of arousal. This is because whilst putting at golf may require a complex mental approach, the muscles will not be working hard and will not therefore need to be highly stimulated. A rugby tackle, or even more so, a weight-lifting exercise, requires less mental activity and more physical arousal. Arousal at cricket will vary somewhat depending on whether the player is bowling – and if so is it fast or slow? - or batting. See Fig. 4.

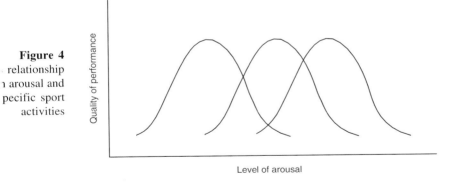

**Figure 4**
relationship
arousal and
pecific sport
activities

The second factor is that the level of arousal will vary depending on the player's level of skill. This may seem to be a little puzzling and the reader might think, Well, they are all playing the same game, aren't they? That is so, but research – and our common sense - shows that a novice will require a lower level of arousal to reach a specific level of performance. The level of performance will drop off as arousal increases, so that if, for example, a batsman has an audience, he is likely to be more anxious and to make more mistakes. At a low level of arousal, the level of performance of the experienced batsman is unlikely to be affected. He will need a much greater level of arousal to reach his peak performance. To understand the reason for this, we have to imagine the early stages of learning a skill – almost any skill. Because the technique will be unfamiliar to us it will not come automatically. As a batsman, we will have to think about the position of the feet, the weight of the body, and the movement of the arms in order to perfect a stroke. As we gain experience, these things will come more naturally. Because the novice has to make a conscious effort to think about his technique, any further arousal is only likely to confuse him. For the experienced player, technique is likely to come automatically; he will need a higher level of arousal to reach his peak performance (see Fig. 5.)

**Figure 5**
Relationship
between level of
arousal and
experience

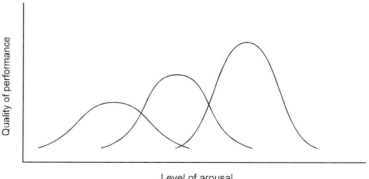

Level of arousal

So what happens when sportsmen engage in their chosen activity? We have just seen that the body's reactions help us when faced with a challenge, so it would be reasonable to assume that these reactions are useful to the cricketer.

Another factor related to arousal is that of attentional focus (see Chapter Eight.) The theory is that when arousal is increased, our attentional field narrows, enabling us to concentrate, and when arousal is at a low level our attentional focus is very broad. When focus is broad, the cricketer can be distracted by irrelevancies – a noisy crowd, a piece of paper fluttering across the pitch, mutterings of other players – and therefore performance is likely to decrease. It follows that if a player is performing alone, his performance is likely to be at a lower level than when performing in front of an audience. When faced with an audience, his arousal level will be higher, and therefore his attentional focus will be narrower – in other words he will be able to concentrate more on the task. However if the audience is highly vocal and animated it is likely to be disruptive of performance, so it seems that there is an optimum level of arousal at which point irrelevancies will be disregarded and concentration will be highest.

John Emburey, spin bowler of Middlesex and England, played in 64 Test matches in spite of having a 6 year ban for playing in South Africa in the 1980s. He had this to say:

*"You block out the crowd noise. You don't notice it. Suddenly, you might hear a hush, and a comment from someone in the crowd. It might be a funny comment, a rude comment, and it may not be aimed at you. That eases the tension. You're more aware of the crowd when it's quiet than when it's noisy. You're very much aware of it when the side is getting wickets and you're bowling and the crowd are behind you. It can be the opposite when you're batting, and the crowd is baying for your blood, and they want you to be out. When you're concentrating your attention is narrowly focused, and when you're not concentrating your attention is broad".*

## Stress

The word 'stress' is used freely and in many different ways. Engineers, doctors and psychologists all use the word 'stress' to mean different things. The word itself is thought to have come into Middle English from the French *destresse*, to be placed under oppression. In English, this became 'distress', and later became separated as 'stress' and 'distress' and carrying different meanings. In this book we shall use the word stress in the sense of having pressure applied. Although the subject of stress has become a popular topic, there seems to be no universal agreement on a definition. Generally, stress can be defined as a state that occurs when people are faced with situations they perceive as threatening and doubt their own ability to deal with these. We interpret the events that the word 'stress' represents in different ways, and it is the manner in which we experience these events which determines whether we find them to be stressful.

The word appears to have negative connotations, but is that necessarily so, and is it all bad? What about people who do not seem to suffer from stress?

Are they more capable than the rest of us? We all know people who seem to take everything in their stride - whether it is an examination or a competitive sport. One wonders whether they have always had that natural advantage or whether they have 'psyched' themselves up for a particular event.

Modern life, with its need to make rapid decisions, its constant need to keep 'ahead of the game', to honour work and family obligations at the same time, perhaps as well as coping with insecurity – all of these factors are likely to produce stress. It is not easy – if it ever was – to satisfy all our objectives. In more primitive communities, survival might still depend on the need to find food and shelter; within our own culture, where these things are largely taken for granted, we are more likely to seek social approval, self respect, and opportunities for advancement. These become the agents of stress for us. It seems that stress has always been with us, and if it isn't there, what do we do? We invent it. Some people leave a job until the last minute, thereby putting themselves under stress, but they will say that they work better – perhaps do their best work - that way. The adrenalin flows and they will get the job done on time. Edgar Wallace, the prolific writer, disciplined himself to write some of his thrillers in a matter of days, to earn money to pay off his gambling debts.

Events that are perceived as threatening are known as *stressors* and our reactions to them are known as *stress responses*. These may be of a physical or psychological nature. Some researchers have concentrated on stressful events, and others have concentrated on our responses to stress, trying to identify our range of reactions to events that are deemed to be threatening or demanding.

When we are blocked in trying to achieve a goal it is likely that stress may result. The irritations can be minor or major. When we are late for an appointment and all the traffic lights are against us, seemingly at every road junction, we are liable to become exasperated. We may be able to control and contain this exasperation by just huffing and puffing, or we may take it out on other road users by driving in a competitive manner, displaying bad road manners, or even 'road rage'. Whenever there is an obstruction between our goal and us, there is the likelihood of stress.

Let us consider the following examples that may be stressful to many of us:

- making a speech *(but I'm a politician, a local councillor, and do this often.)*
- trying to fill in a tax return *(I'm an accountant. What's the problem?)*
- driving a car in central London in the rush hour *(I'm a taxi driver. It's my living.)*
- coping with a computer breakdown *(I run the helpdesk in our company. Love it.)*

Each (or all) of these events might be stressful for a particular individual. It is how that person might perceive the event that determines whether or not it is stressful. A politician should not find making a speech to be stressful, and likewise, an accountant should have no trouble completing a tax return.

We can see therefore, that when we are faced with a potentially stressful situation we do not all respond in the same way. How we respond seems to depend partly on what the nature of the situation might be and partly on our ability to cope with it and to tolerate stress. For example, we might all regard bereavement or a severe illness as being stressful, but for lesser events – when our car breaks down, when we are late for an interview, when we feel we have too much work to do – our responses may vary considerably. Our response to a vehicle breakdown will vary depending perhaps on the extent of our mechanical knowledge and whether we can fix it ourselves. Our reaction to being late for an interview might depend on how badly we want the job, and how important we regard punctuality to be. Having too much work may make us feel inadequate – we feel we ought to be able to manage it but somehow we can't.

When we experience a potentially stressful event we assess the situation at two levels. The first might be to query the significance of the event – What does it mean to me? The second might be, What can I do about it? If we regard the event as stressful then our answer to the second question will depend on a wide range of factors, such as skill, knowledge, previous experience, and material resources.

Stress can best be envisaged as a continuum. At one end we are enlivened by the stress of perhaps meeting a new business contact and wanting to make a good impression, or trying to make an important sale. At the other end we have a degree of stress that might lead to psychological damage if it continues long enough. If we can handle it, we will be stimulated: if not the stress may be damaging. We can see therefore that it is our response to an event that determines whether it is *pleasantly* stressful or *harmfully* stressful.

Transferring this to cricket, we realise that the more important a game might be, the more stressful it might be to a certain type of player. Failure can be seen as damaging to the player's self-esteem, and it is therefore potentially damaging for a coach to overstate the importance of a match – particularly to junior players.

However, one has to be realistic about this. If it is overdone you will be kidding nobody, as the following example shows:

---

In the lead-up to the opening game of the 1999 World Cricket Cup, (England V Sri Lanka), the England coach, David Lloyd said: "We tried as hard as we could to play it down. We told the players to relax, to say to themselves that it was just another one-day international but it was an attempt at kidology. We knew it was a big game and that in a qualifying group it was vital to get off to a good start. And, although the players will deny it until their dying days, they were a bit nervy."

Lloyd later wrote that it took the outside intervention of a Lord's official to achieve in just a few words what he had been attempting for a fortnight. As England warmed up on the outfield before the toss, the Lord's "suit" approached the coach and demanded to know whether he had permission to be there practicing. "That busted the ice," said Lloyd. "The players thought, What? And then they all fell about laughing, they couldn't believe it, it broke everyone down."

---

Some stressful events can be seen as both a challenge and a threat. Being chosen to play for the first eleven may be seen as a challenge ("I've made it!"), and stressful ("I must do well: I mustn't let people down"). Whether it is a challenge or a threat it is still stressful because the player will need to cope with the situation. The main difference is that the challenge is seen as pleasurable and will generate excitement, and the threat may be characterised by the negative emotions of fear and anxiety.

Stress evokes in us a range of physiological responses. Briefly, the muscles demand energy, and extra sugar fuels this need. Our heart rate, blood pressure, and breathing all increase. The air passages to the lungs increase also. Saliva dries up giving us a dry mouth. Endorphins are secreted which act as painkillers, and extra oxygen bearing red blood cells are produced. We are now ready for action in the classic 'fight or flight' response. These reactions are automatic, in the sense that we don't consciously determine them.

Just prior to the 1999 World Cup cricket match between England and Sri Lanka, manager David Graveney warned of emotions getting out of control as a result of a feud the previous winter. He said, "There's a lot of pressure and expectation on us, but if you can control your emotions you can play better." Bob Woolmer made a similar point after his South African team were the victims of two umpiring blunders. "There is nothing we can do about what happens on the field, and under our contracts we can't comment on decisions. It's very important in those situations to remain calm." South Africa went on to win the match. Tennis star Chris Evert, who won 18 Grand Slams, commented on the bad behaviour of Martina Hingis in the final of the French Open, in which she lost to Steffi Graff. Evert said: "I was shocked by what I saw. Martina acted like the teenager she is. She played like a champion but has to learn to behave like one. We have been used to champions like Steffi and Monica Seles keeping their emotions under wraps. But Martina is different. The result showed that if you let your emotions get the better of you, it becomes tough to stay focused and win."

There is a sequel however. Much later in the year, when Hingis was convincingly beaten by Lindsay Davenport, newspapers commented on the remarkable change in Hingis since her "dramatic implosion" at the French Open. The Daily Telegraph commented that "these days she will not be drawn into post-match bickering contests, while on court she has learned to bide her time and keep her temper." It went on, "However being made to look like an also-ran in a showcase final was a little more than she could bear. She slammed down her racket, she hid her face in the towel and looked as if she was ready to fling her toys out of the pram. Still, Hingis is older and marginally wiser than she was in Paris, and she gave it one last go, breaking back to make the first set score respectable." The report concluded that "Hingis was left with a lot of thinking to do over the coming weeks."

Our bodies have responded to the perceived emergency, it has mobilised its resources and is ready for action. When our muscles tense excessively, tasks are not performed as well. We will quickly tire. A three minute judo contest or round of boxing, is utterly exhausting, solely through muscular tension, but doing simple exercises to music with a heavy rhythmic beat, will enable one to carry on easily for twenty minutes or more with little sign of tiredness.

The emotions which stress generates need to be controlled. These emotions can be those of self-doubt, lack of confidence, and insecurity. They are often expressed as anger and almost any Saturday during the football season will produce a crop of examples of players being angry with themselves, the opposition, or the match officials. This affects concentration and in all sport, not least in cricket, concentration is vital.

## Anxiety

Our third term, that of anxiety, now needs to be defined. Anxiety can be either *somatic* or *cognitive*.

Somatic anxiety refers to the physical symptoms we get when anxious, some of which were mentioned earlier, such as sweating, dizziness, hyperventilation, dry mouth, 'butterflies' in the stomach, and perhaps shaky hands. Possible solutions to alleviate somatic anxiety, might be relaxation in a hot bath, sleeping, sex, and massage. Exercise in itself can be relaxing. A work-out at moderate level in a gym will have the affect of releasing some of the brain's chemicals that induce relaxation. 'Jogger's high' is a reality – not just a meaningless phrase.

With cognitive anxiety the solution is more likely to be mental relaxation, and being able to 'switch off', reading, watching television, indulging in a hobby.

Cognitive anxiety refers to mental worries, and particularly to negative thoughts, ("I've never played well on this ground.") There is also an inability to concentrate, and an inability to stop thinking about past or future events in a negative manner.

Anxiety can either be a more or less stable personality trait or characteristic, or it can be purely related to a specific incident or situation, and therefore temporary. As a personality trait, anxiety refers to the extent to which we might be anxious in most situations, and which might generally lead us to be described by those that know us, as an 'anxious person'. Situational anxiety is generated by a specific event or series of events, and will provoke a level of anxiety greater than that which we might normally display. As an example, I recall giving a personality assessment to a player, which indicated that he had a high level of anxiety. This surprised me because I knew him to be a fairly relaxed and easy-going person. In discussing the results with him, I learned that his father had recently died and he felt that the whole family – brothers and sisters – now looked to him for material as well as moral support. He eventually found a way of coping with this, and when I re-assessed him a year later, his anxiety level was where I had expected it to be in the first place - at a reasonably low level. This was a classic example of situational anxiety – a transitory phase that all of us go through at some stage of our lives. It may last for a few hours, a few days, or as in the above case, a few months.

There are in fact several personality characteristics that contribute to a high level of anxiety. These are emotional instability, a high level of self-criticism and apprehension, suspicion of others' motives, and physical tension. Some of these factors are more important than are others[3].

Let us see how an anxiety trait and a situational anxiety state might interact. Someone with a high anxiety trait (a more or less permanent characteristic) will display a *higher level of anxiety* when placed in a stressful situation, than will someone whose anxiety trait is at a lower level. It follows that someone with a naturally low level of anxiety will display *a lower level of anxiety* when placed in an equally stressful situation.

Let us now transfer these two concepts – that of situational anxiety and trait anxiety - into the cricketing context. The level of stress that the cricketer actually experiences will depend to a large extent on what he can bring to the situation - ability, and knowledge of similar situations in the past, will be two of the factors. A third might be his ability to manage stress – and it is this, which might distinguish the successful player from the rest. Clearly, a cricketer who has additional responsibilities needs to be able to manage the additional stress also.

Hampshire's captain and former Test player, Robin Smith, in an interview just before the opening of the 1999 World Cricket Cup, had this to say about the responsibilities on the shoulders of the England captain and wicket keeper Alec Stewart: "He's too good a player for this to go on [commenting on Stewart's lack of recent form]. "But maybe he has too much on his plate and too many things to think about other than his batting. Even at this level, as a county captain, my workload is huge, so it must be a hundred times worse for him. I wouldn't wish it on my worst enemy."

John Emburey has added his own comments to those of Robin Smith:

*"Alec was happy to play all those roles, but it was felt that it affected his game, so he either had to get rid of the gloves, or bat down the order, or give up the captaincy.   I'm sure playing all those roles did affect his form, and if it affects your form then it devalues your worth in the side.  The most important thing for the team was for Alec to be the all-rounder, to keep wicket, to bat and get runs."*

Jack Birkenshaw says that there might be many reasons for a player to feel anxious. *"You might be anxious to get a score because the England selectors are watching you. It might be because you want another contract next year. You might want a good score because your bat manufacturer may reward you.  Maybe you're anxious because you're facing a bowler who's got you out year after year.  The coach has got to spend time with the player. As a batsman you've got to go out there and make that anxiety work for you.  Realise you're anxious, realise you're nervous and worried, and when you get out there, keep calm, breathe deeply, and focus on one ball at a time.*

Michael Vaughan was formerly captain of the England A and U-19 sides so he has been tipped as a possible future England captain. He made his Test debut against South Africa in the winter tour of 1999 – 2000, and when he walked out to bat he had just seen two dismissals and England were 5 for 2.  And Allan Donald and Shaun Pollock were bowling!  Did it worry Vaughan?  He said: *"There are a lot of nerves before going out to bat but, as soon as I walk out, I tell myself that it's just another game of cricket with a red ball coming down at me from the other end.  I'm not the type to get wound up in traffic jams or anything.  Only when Sheffield Wednesday are losing."*

The supreme example of stress management in recent cricketing lore, must have been Australian captain Steve Waugh's magnificent innings of 120 to defeat South Africa by 5 wickets at Headingley in the World Cup. When he walked to the wicket, Australia seemed doomed at 48 – 3 chasing South Africa's 271. If Australia lost, they would be on the next plane home instead of moving on to the semi-finals. South Africa were already guaranteed a place in the semi-finals. In true Boys Own Paper-style Waugh defied the might of

South Africa's Pollock and Donald and at the last over of the day the Australians still had to get 8 runs to win – which they did, of course. Afterwards, Waugh said, "Hundreds don't come along that often when you're batting five or six. Making one under pressure, that's something I've dreamt of doing."

According to Davies and Armstrong[4] a consistent research finding among sportsmen shows that anxiety levels are at their highest immediately before a game, but once the match has started, anxiety levels decrease. As always, the waiting is the worst part. Anxiety levels are likely to rise therefore, from the day before a match, through to the morning of the match, arriving at the ground, and changing in the dressing room. In physically demanding sports it is known that anxiety levels fall sharply, whilst in goalkeeping, golf, high jumping, and archery, all of which require less energy, competitors can remain tense and anxious throughout the contest. For the batsman, it is arguably worse than this because he will have to wait until a wicket has fallen – which could mean hours of waiting in a three, four, or five day match – and then he has to be ready to take his place at the wicket within two minutes of that wicket falling. Once at the wicket, the more energy that is dissipated, the quicker will the anxiety be relieved, but we know that the tactics of the game might well demand that the batsman simply 'keeps his end up', thus providing little opportunity to relieve tension. It is thought that this tension might be the reason why some suffer from a serious loss of form. Vigorous exercise beforehand would alleviate the tension.

Does an anxious player perform better than does the player with a lower level of anxiety? Infuriatingly perhaps, there is no simple answer to this. Research seems to indicate that there are 'cut-off points' in a scale of anxiety above and below which performance is likely to suffer. The actual level of anxiety will vary according to the player's ability and his own perception of that ability. Therefore a player of high ability is less likely to be anxious if he has evaluated his chances of success and has come to a positive conclusion, ("I know I can win.") A player of lower ability will see his chances of success as lower, and is therefore likely to be more anxious, ("I'm not sure I'm good enough to be in this side.") Because he is more anxious, his performance is likely to suffer.

Anxiety is closely related to confidence and self-efficacy, which is discussed in detail in Chapter Nine. An anxious player is likely to blame himself for defeat, perhaps believing that he is lacking in ability. A less anxious player is more likely to attribute blame to a lack of effort. "I only have to practice a bit more and I'll be OK", might sum up his attitude. Each of these attitudes fuels itself. The anxious player who fails will blame himself and believe there is little he can do about it. The more confident player will practice more, which in turn is more likely to lead to success.

We have seen that an anxious competitor may fare worse than will a more stable one when the importance of an event is over-emphasised, but it is also true that the more anxious competitor is likely to have more difficulty in adjusting to unusual conditions. Anxious competitors may have a tendency towards inflexibility making their actions somewhat predictable. The anxious cricketer therefore has much to contend with if he is to make progress. How can he be helped?

A good starting point of course, might be with younger players. Research has shown that they can become conditioned into feeling anxious whilst competing, highlighting the importance as mentioned elsewhere, of the need for the coach to emphasise the importance of *enjoyment and fun*. There is no need for enjoyment and competition to be mutually exclusive – certainly not for young cricketers.

No chapter on stress and anxiety in sport would be complete without some reference to the effect that an audience can have on a player. A number of sport psychologists have conducted much research into this subject, most going back to the 1930s, although the earliest study was in 1897. Robert Zajonc (pronounced zion) has conducted the most influential studies into audience effect, and his work examines the consequences on the sportsman's behaviour of the sheer presence of other people.

One of Zajonc's key findings was that a simple or well-learned response was helped by the presence of spectators, but with a new response in the presence of spectators, the performance was impaired. He concluded that the presence of others is psychologically arousing and it is this that produces the 'dominant response'. (This theory has much appeal and might come under the heading of a 'common sense' theory, but psychologists still need to test and validate such theories if psychology is to be regarded as a science.) Now let's transfer Zajonc's findings to cricket. What he is saying is that if, for example a cricketer is learning a new stroke – let's say the square cut – his performance might suffer if others are watching him. His dominant response will be to play the stroke as best he can, and for a beginner that is unlikely to be a polished stroke. However an experienced cricketer is likely to benefit from the presence of an audience, because the audience will have the effect of increasing his arousal.

The significance of this last sentence is that the coach needs to handle the young cricketer with tact and sensitivity if he is to get the best results from him. Even a learner talented as batsman or bowler, will tend to make mistakes when aroused in the psychological sense, and the coach should be instrumental in encouraging an attitude of acceptance of this, on the part of the young player. Feedback is of two types – positive and negative – and we all know which we prefer, but the young player needs to be encouraged to see constructive criticism as an aid to improved performance. How else can we learn?

As stated, the experienced cricketer should be helped – or at least not handicapped – by the presence of an audience. The coach should look for situations that present opportunities for the experienced player to shine under pressure. For example, if it is imperative that your side gets a wicket before lunch, you would need not just to select your best bowler, but the *best bowler who has been in that situation before.* (Obvious? Maybe, but remember the extra time penalty kick taken in the 1998 World Cup by England's David Batty who had never been asked to take a penalty before? He missed.)

Another principle arising from Zajonc's work is that sports (or tasks) which rely on simple speed and power are made easier through the presence of an audience. This is because a greater level of arousal is required for 'tough' tasks and the audience can help the sportsman to achieve this. Consider the level of arousal required for a golfer and a weight lifter. Consider the audience effect on the contenders in the televised World's Strongest Man competition.

Anxiety at some level is a given in competitive sport. The apparent remedies to control – but not eliminate it – are relaxation, visualisation, and imagery. We deal with these in the next chapter. Positive self-talk and affirmations – other remedies – are included in Chapter Nine.

# CHECK LIST FOR AROUSAL, STRESS AND ANXIETY

❖ These characteristics are closely related.

❖ Arousal deals with the physiological response that occurs when we are faced with a situation that we perceive to be potentially stressful. The main physical symptoms are an increased heart rate, heavy breathing, sweating, trembling, and "butterflies" in the stomach.

❖ A high level of arousal has the effect of narrowing attentional focus, and a low level of arousal broadens it, making it more difficult to concentrate.

❖ Stress is the name we give to our reaction to an event that appears to be daunting or challenging or threatening, and we doubt our own ability to deal with it. The events are known as *stressors*, and our responses to them are known as *stress responses*. Although stress is perceived as negative, a low level of stress may act as sufficient spur to increase our performance. A high level of stress may be detrimental to our performance.

❖ Anxiety can be somatic or cognitive. Somatic anxiety refers to the physical symptoms we experience when we are anxious – e.g. sweating, dizziness, dry mouth, etc. Cognitive anxiety refers to our negative state of mind, and an inability to concentrate.

❖ Anxiety can also be classified as situational or as a characteristic trait. Situational anxiety is of short-term duration: of hours, weeks or months. Trait anxiety refers to a personality characteristic that is a permanent feature of our make-up.

❖ Cricket coaches need to be aware that an audience can increase arousal, having a detrimental affect on a beginner, but acting as a stimulus to an experienced player.

❖ Stress management encompasses several techniques such as positive self-talk, imagery, relaxation, and visualisation.

# 6    Relaxation

*Cricket is the queerest game,*
*Every stroke is just the same –*
*Merely whacking at a ball;*
*Nothing else to see at all.*
*Then there comes a big surprise*
*When I chance to close my eyes.*

*A Queer Game.*
Anon

England cricketer Alan Mullally is well known for being 'laid back' even more than is the illustrious David Gower. Perhaps the pinnacle of 'laid-backness' was reached when a laconic Western Australian and Leicestershire fast bowler, Graham McKenzie, once failed to leave the field for a lunch break at Grace Road because he had fallen asleep on his feet at third man!

Andy Flintoff, the Lancashire and England right-hand batsman was asked what he felt like having been picked for the World Cup squad at the early age of 21 years. "I'm pretty relaxed," he said, not at all fazed that he would be the youngster of the team. "I'll just go out there, do my best, and enjoy it."

As we saw in the last chapter, tension and anxiety are almost always self-induced. It is not the situation as such that is the cause of the worry, but the way we perceive it, and our response to that.

Of course, anxiety cannot be entirely eliminated – nor should it be. A certain amount of stress is what enables us to put in that bit extra, to meet the deadline, to be completely alert, to be ready for action. What we are concerned with is not the elimination of anxiety but the ability to control it, to minimise it, so that it works in our favour by enhancing performance, rather than diminishing it. Remember the connection between physical arousal, which if too low, will lead to a second rate performance, and if too high may lead to the same. There are physical and mental dimensions to relaxation and here, we shall deal with them both.

## Physical relaxation

Like other sportsmen, cricketers can learn to relax their bodies, and there are well-established techniques for doing this. The skills are not difficult to acquire, but they do need to be practised regularly and systematically and the cricket coach can be very influential in this regard. With regular practice, the cricketer is more likely to be able to relax at will.

Physical relaxation is valuable but many of us find that we are soon tense again, once the relaxation session is over. This is because we are unaware of the muscular tension in our bodies. We do not listen to our bodies, but ignore the symptoms and then wonder why we have a splitting headache – perhaps because we have allowed the neck muscles to tighten. Tightening of the muscles is the body's way of preparing for action, and when that action is not forthcoming, the energy is not properly discharged. The 16 Personality Factor Questionnaire (16PF5) referred to elsewhere, can clearly identify a candidate's level of physical tension, and high scorers report irritability, impatience, and muscle tightness. In a word, tension. We know that we can discharge the tension through physical activity but it is often difficult to do this – our environment may not allow it – and because of this, by the end of the day, our muscles may be tight as a drum. How often have you sat in a chair for a long period, only half-aware that the neck muscles and those around the shoulders are tight? They have been ready for action - but they had no work to do. To avoid this, we need to release the tension when it arises, and we can do this by developing an awareness of tension in our bodies. Telling the muscles that action is not necessary can dispel contraction of the muscles, which have been prepared for action. Initially, this will be a conscious decision, but with practice it will become the norm, and relaxation will become habitual.

Our breathing operates on a similar basis. We tend to hold our breath when we have some physical exertion and even in an argument we might hold our breath waiting to make a comment. What happens? Our comments may be short, staccato, and less articulate than we had rehearsed them! When we become more aware of our bodies, we learn to recognise these symptoms immediately and do something about them.

These points emphasise that relaxation is not something that the cricketer should practice only before a vital match. It should be part of his normal waking routine and the coach has an influential part to play in encouraging this amongst his team.

It seems that some types of relaxation technique suit some people more than others, and coaches and cricketers can experiment between the following examples to find which suits them best.

One technique for relaxation includes the following stages[1]

- Find a quiet place where you are unlikely to be disturbed. Lie on your bed or on the floor.
- Cover yourself lightly so that you are warm.
- Tense and then relax the muscles in your right foot and ankle.
- Do this several times and remember how it felt.
- Do the same with the left foot and ankle. Do it several times and remember how it felt.
- Do the same with the calf muscles. Tense and relax them, first the right leg then the left. Feel the difference between clenching and relaxing.
- Do the same with the thigh muscles.
- Do the same with the buttocks.
- Now move to the back. Relax the back deeply. Feel how good it is when it is relaxed. Remember the difference.
- Now move to the stomach, then the chest. Tighten and then relax the muscles on each occasion.
- Now do the same with the shoulders, arms, and wrists.
- Now move to the jaw, face, and scalp.

Alternatively coaches might like to practice the following technique and train their cricketers to do likewise. This technique is known as progressive relaxation and was originally developed in 1938 by E. Jacobson. It is one of the most popular methods of relaxation, being simple to use, although regular practice is required.

1. Sit quietly in a comfortable position and close your eyes.
2. Deeply relax all your muscles, beginning at your feet and progressing to your face. Keep them deeply relaxed.
3. Breath through your nose. Become aware of your breathing. As you breathe out, say the word "one" silently to yourself. For example, breathe in … out, "one"; in … out, "one" and so on. Continue for 20

minutes. You may open your eyes to check the time, but do not use an alarm. When you finish, sit quietly for several minutes at first with closed eyes and later with opened eyes.

4. Do not worry about whether you are successful in achieving a deep level of relaxation. Maintain a passive attitude and permit relaxation to occur at its own pace. Expect other thoughts. When these distracting thoughts occur, shrug them off and continue repeating "one". With practice, the response should come with little effort.

5. Practice the technique once or twice daily but not within two hours after a meal, since the digestive processes seem to interfere with the subjective changes.[2]

If the cricket coach wishes to teach this method in a group, the following instructions can be used[3.]

## Say:

*Make yourself comfortable... remove watches, glasses and shoes...uncross your arms and your legs... close your eyes. Breathe slowly and deeply...slowly and deeply. Focus your attention on your right foot and ankle...when I give you the word, tense the muscles in your right foot and ankle. Ready...NOW.*

While tensing say: *"Feel the tension... feel the muscles pulling...Hold it for 7 seconds... RELAX.*

While relaxing say: *" Feel the tension drain away... let the muscles relax... that feels good...relax more and more...you feel much more relaxed than you did before...carry on relaxing...feel how pleasant it is...you are now feeling more and more relaxed...feel how relaxed the muscles are now...you are calm and rested...* (Approximate length 30 seconds.)

Now repeat the tension and relaxation routine again for the left foot and ankle.

## Say:

*When I give the signal tense your left foot and ankle...NOW. Hold it for 7 seconds. RELAX.*

Repeat the phrases for tensing as above.

Continue through calf muscles, thighs, buttocks, back, stomach, shoulders, and chest. Then move to the jaw face and scalp. Using the tensing phrases and the relaxation phrases for each set of muscles.

When the exercises have been completed count back from seven to one. On the count of SEVEN move your feet, on SIX, your legs, FIVE your buttocks, FOUR your back, THREE your shoulders, TWO your neck, and ONE your face.

Now open your eyes get up, and move around slowly.

When the coach is thoroughly familiar with these techniques, he might like to record them on tape, and make it available to the team.

## Mental relaxation

Most of us like to use our imagination to re-create situations we have experienced. We can remember scenes in great detail. One technique that is often coupled with relaxation is that of visualisation. Some writers use this word as being synonymous with mental rehearsal, mental practising, or imagery, to name just a few. In this chapter we are using the word to describe a mental process that the cricketer can use to help calm the mind.

- Visualise a scene with which you are very familiar and which is pleasant and relaxing – certainly it should be reassuring and have happy associations. It might be a beach scene, a garden, a favourite countryside view – anything that the cricketer finds pleasant. Some people find this easier to do than others. If it doesn't come easily, don't worry. Just do the best you can.
- When you have established the scene, look for details. It might be the colour of flowers in the garden, the blue

of the sea, a deserted beach. The colours may not be vivid, but that won't matter. If the visualisation begins to slip, don't let that worry you. Try to get as much detail as possible into your vision.

- Now let that vision fade away and replace it with another – perhaps one of those mentioned above, or something completely different. It may be a house that has many happy memories for you or a mountain stream. As long as it is peaceful, reassuring, and pleasant, it does not matter.

- When the details are clear imagine yourself as part of the scene. Imagine *drifting into* that scene and being part of it. Imagine the sand on the beach, or the blue of the water, or the sun on your back.

- Try to identify with the peacefulness of the scene. Imagine that there are no pressures to do anything, no objectives, and no obligations. You are just content to be part of the scene.

- Stay as part of the scene for at least five minutes, but longer if you so wish. Eventually, you need to allow the scene to fade, and gradually come back to the present. Don't be in a hurry to do this; do it gradually, then open your eyes and come back to the present.

---

Let the tranquillity you have achieved remain with you. Don't start anything physically or mentally strenuous straightaway. Be aware of the new-found relaxation and let this become uppermost in your thoughts as you begin to pick up where you left off.

Remember that all of this requires practice. Don't be disappointed if it doesn't work for you the first time. You are probably trying to overcome years of habitual stress! It can't be done in a few moments, but it is worthwhile pursing in order to enjoy greater relaxation and effectiveness.

# CHECK LIST FOR RELAXATION

❖ Relaxation is a skill that can be learned.

❖ It needs to be encouraged by the coach and practised regularly, becoming part of a daily routine for the cricketer.

❖ Physical relaxation can be achieved through planned exercises

❖ Our muscles tense even when they have no work to do.

❖ Mental relaxation can be practised separately or integrated with the exercises for physical relaxation.

❖ Imagine a pleasant and relaxing scene, but don't worry if you find this difficult at first. It will become easier with practice.

# 7    Mental rehearsal

*Willow and cane, nothing but that –*
*O, but it's glorious swinging the bat!*
*Leather and thread, there you have all –*
*O, but it's glorious gripping the ball!*

*Good Days*
E. V. Lucas

The cricket correspondent of the Daily Telegraph was scathing.

*"Psychologists, I ask you," he wrote. "How many wickets have they ever taken? The coach as king is a bridge too far. Sometimes, with all the nonsense spoken these days of 'focus' and 'visualisation', one wonders how all those terrible players, the Huttons, and the Comptons, the Bedsers and the Truemans, the Bothams, for crying out loud, ever raised a gallop."*

The sport psychologist might very reasonably reply that taking wickets is not part of his remit – but helping other people to take them is! Perhaps that particular correspondent has come round to thinking that there must be something in it after all, because five months later, at the start of England's tour of South Africa, he reflected on Atherton's greatness as a cricketer, recalling his 1995 score of 185 against South Africa as one of the greatest innings of all time. And he quoted Atherton as saying:

*"I've got a video of that innings. It is one of the four or five that I've got on tape that I use to see how my game has developed, and to reaffirm my confidence in my ability when I'm low. There's one against New Zealand in 1990, when I first came into the team, a hundred I made at Guyana on my first tour I made as captain, and another against Australia. It's a little artificial tool to give myself a bit of confidence occasionally. Funnily enough, I don't recall too much about it. I remember being dropped at short leg on 99, bringing up my hundred with a pull and playing a few straight drives.*

*But I was concentrating so hard on batting that most details are beyond me. After playing an innings like that you're always trying to replicate what it felt like, and the most difficult innings of all is the one that follows it.*

*Clinically, I think I played well that day, and the captaincy certainly brought a bit extra out of me, but I think I'm playing better now. Technically, I don't think I was playing at my best, but I got through on a mixture of determination, courage, steadfastness, call it what you like. Johannesburg can be a pretty intimidating place to play. In that context it was a good effort."*

There is plenty of evidence – documentary as well as anecdotal – showing that mental rehearsal works.

Golfer Jack Nicklaus developed the technique of mental rehearsal on his own, years ago[1]. He wrote:

*I never a hit shot, even in practice, without having a sharp, in-focus picture of it in my head. It's like a colour movie. First, I "see" the ball where I want it to finish, nice and white and sitting high up on the bright green grass. Then the scene quickly changes, and I 'see' the ball going there: its path, trajectory, and shape, even its behaviour on landing. Then there's a sort of fade out, and the next swing shows me making the kind of swing that will turn the previous images into reality. Only at the end of this short, private, Hollywood spectacular, do I select a club and step up to the ball.*

If the cricket coach needs further evidence of the power of mental rehearsal, listen to David Hemery, Olympic gold medallist, and world record holder for the 400m hurdles[2]:

*"It struck me that the first four-minute mile by Sir Roger Bannister had first to be mentally conceived as possible, similarly for man to walk on the moon, it had to be thought of as a serious possibility. All that then remained was the hours of dedication and intelligent application of time, effort and resources to achieve the goal! The thought helped me in my own quest of bettering what had been done before in my event of*

> *400m hurdles. In the months prior to the Olympic Games, apart from the hours of physical practice, many more hours were spent mentally rehearsing the effort distribution, pace judgement, stride pattern and hurdling technique for a successful attempt to break the existing world record, which I hoped to be good enough to win the Olympics. Even while lying down, the visualisation was so clear that my pulse rate and breathing would come close to what I would actually experience in a race".*

Hemery states that 80% of the world's top sports people, whom he interviewed, said that they used visualisation and mental rehearsal as an aid.

In answer to the question, "To what extent was the mind involved in playing your sport?" the unanimous verdict was "totally", "immensely", "you play with your mind", and "that's where the body movement comes from."

Let's conduct a little experiment to see in what way the mind can influence the body.

Stand up, close your eyes, and imagine you are on the top of a very high building. A skyscraper perhaps. The roof is very small in area. You are standing near the edge of a very low parapet. You look down hundreds of feet onto the pavement below. Hold that vision for a few seconds. What are your sensations?

Queasy stomach? Nausea? Giddiness? A feeling of vulnerability, perhaps? The point is that you *can* create physical sensations using the mind. Creating happy and successful occasions may take slightly more effort, but it can be done with practice.

The process of mental rehearsal has the effect of allowing the cricketer to 'feel what it is like' to practice a specific shot, or to bowl in certain conditions. He needs to practice the movements to be as near perfect as possible. When he is in competition therefore, he will have the valuable feeling of having 'been there before'. He will have the knowledge that his technique can be improved; this will increase his self-esteem and therefore his confidence.

Jack Birkenshaw says that practising a shot seemed to be more prevalent many years ago. *"You'd stand in front of the mirror and practice your shot. If you'd watched some of the great players of yesteryear, you'd have seen them practising their shots all the while. It needs to be habit-forming, part of that player's preparation."*

Let's take another example:

> *"The camera zooms in on a figure clad from head to toe*
> *in space-age synthetic material, racing helmet in place,*
> *poles gripped firmly in each hand.  As the camera*
> *brings us closer, we see that her eyes are closed; her*
> *body is swaying from side to side; and although she is*
> *standing in one spot, her movements suggest that she is*
> *skiing down a steep, snow-covered slope, her body*
> *twisting and her arms moving as if reacting to dangerous*
> *turns and icy patches.  The announcer's voice*
> *interrupts, saying, "And there is the favourite, waiting*
> *her turn in the starting order.  You can see her mentally*
> *picturing her entire run now, from the starting gate to*
> *the finishing line.  Just* look *at her concentration!"* [3].

No doubt we have all seen this type of scene on television when watching a sporting event. Many, like golfer Jack Nicklaus, have spoken about the manner in which imagery has helped them to be consistently successful.

But let's start at the beginning.  What actually is mental rehearsal, and can it really help the sportsman towards an improved performance?

To quote Spinoza, "If you wish to argue with me, first define your terms."

Mental rehearsal is often referred to as imagery, but other terms are mental practising, symbolic rehearsal, dreams, hallucinations, modelling, hypnosis, and confusingly, visualisation.

In this book, we shall stick to the term 'mental rehearsal'. This is the process of *mimicking* sensory or perceptual experiences and is a purely mental function. The individual is aware of these experiences and the images are not produced by any stimulus. In this way, the skier referred to above, can imagine what it is like to ski, without the stimulus of the ski slope, the mountain or the snow.

Mental practising allows the player to successfully produce mentally, a specific skill – let's say a batsman producing a back-foot drive.

Many sportsmen have long believed that the only way to acquire a motor skill is through long hours of repetition.  In no sport was this idea more prevalent than in judo. How many young judo players gave up the sport because they were sick and tired of beating the dust out of the mats in an attempt at learning how to break-fall! Not only is this type of activity boring, but it crushes creativity and leads to a sort of blind, unquestioning obedience that 'this is the way you do it', thereby stifling attempts to experiment. This is the very opposite to the 'learning by discovery' method which, for the right player, can be so powerful and which encourages creativity.

Many research experiments have taken place dating back to the 1930s with the earliest in 1892. Some of the results were inconclusive but one researcher in the early 1980s concluded that mental practice when combined and alternated with physical practice is more effective than either alone. So a cricketer imagining himself playing a forward defensive shot is better than not imagining it at all, but going to the nets and practising the shot when combined with mental rehearsal, would be even better. Perhaps South African cricketer Lance Klusner, famous for what has been called his 'agricultural shot', combines mental rehearsal with practice. Practice? Oh yes, up to one hour a day. (Strange to think that at the age of 13 he was dropped from his school team for 'blocking'!)

The reader might wonder whether the process of mental practising has been used outside sport. The answer is that it has, and in the 1980s a researcher investigated the use of mental practice to enhance the musical performance of college trombonists! He found that physical practice combined with mental practice produced the best results. Other researchers have come to similar conclusions.

Another aspect of mental rehearsal refers to its use just prior to competition, and usually referred to as 'psyching up'. A study in the 1970s amongst 30 weightlifters showed that the 15 who used their usual psyching up strategies performed better than the other 15 who were given a distracting mental task to perform immediately before their performance. The successful psyching-up strategies included positive self-talk, control of attention, preparatory arousal and visualisation. However, we know very little about *how* this actually improves performance.

One psychotherapist who works with sportsmen says[4]:

> *"[Sportsmen] are already highly motivated and are working towards achievable goals. A psychologist can always help an athlete improve their performance. The top 100 golfers are each capable of great things - on their day. The difference between number 1 and number 100 is whether they produce their best performances consistently under the stress of competition."* He went on to say that he worked with

> *the Welsh national archery squad, which was able to produce great scores in practice, but not in competition. The players learned to use three different techniques – mental rehearsal, controlled breathing, and biofeedback enabling them to reduce their heart rate when they needed to shoot.*
>
> *He said that mental rehearsal is an important way of boosting confidence and motivation. The archers practised bringing on a particular mental state by associating it with an image they can readily call to mind. They used images of stable objects – such as a boulder – to enable them to keep steady as they prepared to shoot. When these images are routinely used to conjure up the feeling of steadiness in practice, when there is no pressure, they will retain their effectiveness under the stress of competition.*

Mental rehearsal was also used amongst male gymnasts in the 1976 US Olympic team. Six gymnasts only could be chosen from a squad of 13 who were all assessed on such characteristics as anxiety, personality traits and thinking style. Those eventually chosen were found to be more self confident, thought more about gymnastics in everyday situations, and practised mental rehearsal more frequently.

Given that a group of sportsmen practice mental rehearsal, and have the same level of sporting ability, would their performances differ, and if so why? Several researchers have reported that the better performers have greater *vividness* and *controllability* of their visualisation. The studies related to racquetball players, to divers, and to a group of Canadian male Olympic athletes. It seems that internal mental rehearsal is likely to lead to more success than will external mental rehearsal, since one researcher found that skiers who rehearsed *themselves* skiing (external) were less successful than skiers who visualised themselves from an *internal aspect,* in which they imagined what their muscles would feel like during performance.

The vast majority of studies have concerned positive visualisation. But if this seems to work for many people, it would seem logical that the reverse, negative visualisation would produce failure. This was put to the test in the early 1970s using a dart-throwing task, in which the subjects were told to mentally rehearse the movements but to imagine failure as the outcome. The researcher found that the negative thinking downgraded the performance. In the same way that positive visualisation is not easily explained in terms of its affects on improving performance, so it is equally difficult to identify precisely why negative thinking results in a lowering of performance.

The link between certain mental operations and involuntary muscular movements has been the subject of many studies dating back as far as 1892. These studies have noted that there is activity in the muscles similar to that which would occur in actual movement, "but at a lesser magnitude".

Given that visualisation is generally regarded by sport psychologists to be a positive aid to performance, in what other areas might we use this technique? There seem to be three areas worthy of attention. These are in skill acquisition, in skill maintenance and in arousal.

There is strong evidence to suggest that mental practice can help in acquiring a new skill, particularly if the player has had some practical experience first. There seem to be two ways in which to acquire a new motor skill. According to some writers[5], the first is *verbal* and *analytical*, and the second is *intuitive* and *global*. It is the second method that appears to be best. The writers use the example of the golf swing: in the early stages one's attention had to be spread over the many elements of the swing – position of the feet, hands, arms, head, etc. The result would probably be a poor representation of the proper way to swing the club. This is known as the molecular approach. At a much later stage the golfer would automatically adopt the correct stance and the skill would seem to come 'automatically'. Perhaps visualisation techniques could be used to hasten this progress? The writers go on to conjecture about the use of imagery techniques by children to acquire motor skills. This would seem to be a fertile area in which schools' cricket coaches could experiment.

Once the skill has been acquired, it needs to be maintained of course, and mental rehearsal can help in this regard. What is not known, is whether a skill once learned, could be maintained by mental practice alone over a long period.

A most important factor with mental rehearsal – as with relaxation techniques that also use imagery – is that of practice. One psychologist[6] proposed the following steps for mental rehearsal.

1. Find a quiet place. Move into a comfortable position and relax.
2. Visualise a circle that fills the visual field. Make the circle turn a deep blue. Repeat the process several times,

     imagining a different colour each time. Allow the images to disappear. Relax and observe the spontaneous imagery that arises.

3. Create the image of a simple three-dimensional glass. Fill it with a colourful liquid, add ice cubes and a straw. Write a descriptive caption underneath.

4. Select a variety of scenes and develop them with rich detail. Include a cricket pitch, and perhaps a swimming pool, or a golf course. Practice visualising people in these scenes – some whom you know, others as strangers.

5. Imagine yourself in a cricket scene. Visualise your favourite batting stroke, or your bowling technique, or some other activity that you wish to accomplish perfectly. Every time and with ease. Relax and enjoy your success.

6. End the session by breathing deeply, opening your eyes, and adjusting to your surroundings.

---

Galton who was interested in the differing abilities of individuals to use imagery first studied this in the 1880s. Much work has been done in recent years, and in fact there is a Journal of Mental Imagery. Nonetheless, we still know relatively little about how imagery as used in mental rehearsal actually works and some of the research is contradictory. It seems that it has more value in sports that require cognitive – thinking – skills. More useful in cricket, tennis or golf, than in tug-o'-war, perhaps.

On a practical note, one can say that whilst there may be disagreement amongst sport academics about the value of imagery in mental rehearsal, the facts are that a large number of top competitors use it regularly. It seems on this count alone, it is worth while for the cricket coach to encourage his players to use it.

# CHECK LIST FOR MENTAL REHEARSAL

❖ A large percentage of the world's top sportsmen use mental rehearsal as a preparation technique for skill improvement and for competition.

❖ Mental rehearsal entails forming mental images of successful applications of a skill.

❖ Mental rehearsal using external images allows the player to see himself performing a skill. Internal imagery allows the player to experience the skill kinaesthetically. A player should develop the ability to use both internal and external images for mental rehearsal.

❖ The skilled and experienced player is likely to benefit more from the use of imagery. The coach should ensure that the young cricketer knows what proper execution of the skill looks like and feels like *before* encouraging him to use imagery for mental rehearsal.

❖ Mental rehearsal should not simply be a visual picture, but a total recreation of a skill.

# 8    Attentional focus and style

*"I can claim to have been present when a flying bomb, passing overhead at Lord's failed to distract the attention of either the players or the spectators from the game in hand; though I have to confess that as I was unable to hear either planes or sirens, I knew nothing about the incident till I read it in the papers the next morning."*

A *Deaf Man Looks at Cricket*
David Wright

"He lost his concentration." Sports writers frequently attribute this failure not just to cricketers, but tennis stars, footballers, boxers, and just about any sports person who loses a match or game. For sporting success, concentration is a prerequisite. Can it be that anyone playing at this level is unmindful of that? Hardly. And how do we know when someone is concentrating and when not? Were the brows of such cricketing greats as David Gower, Derek Randall, always furrowed in concentration? Clearly not. David Gower was famous for his 'laid-back' style; Derek Randall loved to play the clown, although outside the game this was not his usual demeanour. Gower and Randall both accumulated an incredible amount of runs if they weren't concentrating. So there must be something else at work here.

Brilliant Australian all-rounder Gregg Chappell had a special technique to help him concentrate. He has said, "When batting it was when the bowler turned at the top of his run. I would concentrate until nothing further could happen – until we had taken our runs or we'd established that there would be no more runs from that ball. Then I'd switch off until the bowler got back to his line. If you concentrated the whole time you'd be mentally exhausted." [1] Chappell said that he focused on the face of the bowler until the bowler reached his delivery stride. "Then I'd look for the ball and then the hand and try to watch it come round, particularly focusing on where the bowler was going to let the ball go. You're picking up the angle the ball leaves the hand, your brain reacts to the length and line from the down and sideways angles, giving you a fraction of a second to react. Eyesight's not important, it's reaction." [2]

---

Ian Botham admitted having the same type of ability to concentrate – to be able to switch it on or off as necessary. Arnold Palmer and Lee Trevino were able to laugh and joke with the crowd between shots during which they concentrated 100%, but clearly Colin Montgomerie is unable to do this, and in 1999 American spectators discovered his weakness and capitalised on it to Montgomerie's detriment.

The ability to concentrate and pay attention to something specific in our environment has long been of interest to psychologists as far back as the 1890s. We know that it is a skill that can be acquired and developed. It has been of particular interest to sport psychologists, given that the ability to concentrate is key to any sport. Whether fielding, bowling or batting, the cricketer will need to concentrate. The ability to do this, combined of course with the requisite skill, is one of the factors that separate the great from the also-ran. One has only to think of South African Jonty Rhodes, perhaps the best fielder in the world today, and Geoff Boycott when at his peak, with his ability to stay at the wicket for hours. Concentration involves the ability to focus on the matter in hand to the exclusion of all else. When Mike Atherton scored his 13th Test century playing against South Africa, a newspaper report said: "To observe Atherton throughout the innings in which he helped his side to avoid the follow-on, was to watch a man able to detach from the dark consequences of failure, perfectly at home with his trade, and without an extraneous thought in his head. Indeed so clear was his focus on matters in hand, that he was able to brush off the attempts of Jonty Rhodes to distract him with some chat and a white handkerchief … as just childish nonsense."

To put this in context, we have only to think of the attentional span required of say, a high jumper, a sprinter, or a footballer, which might be 15 seconds, 10 seconds, and 90 minutes respectively. Cricket at Test level is unique in that it requires concentration over 5 days and the ability to be at the crease for many hours. Even at the amateur and 'village' level, concentration may be required for several hours. And yet we know that it is a physical impossibility to concentrate

96

100% for anything like this length of time. School lessons are usually 40 minutes long. Television adverts span less than a minute because advertisers know that most people have the attentional span of a gnat. The cricketer can only achieve long spells at batting or bowling through being able to switch constantly from concentration to relaxation. Any televised cricket match will show the batsman returning to concentration as the bowler begins his run-up, followed by relaxation and a change of attention when the ball has been played.

In sport, we are concerned particularly with *selectivity* and *alertness*.

Selectivity is the ability to pay attention to one specific issue. A batsman needs to concentrate on the delivery of the ball if he is to defend his wicket successfully. But equally, he needs to be able to switch from a narrow focus to that of a wide focus. The fielder needs to concentrate on the batsman's stroke and try to anticipate the direction and flight of the ball. The bowler will need to concentrate on the ball, but between deliveries he will need to study the position of the fielders, as well as the condition of the pitch and the weather.

Selectivity implies that we can only focus on one thing at a time. But is this true? Clearly not. When we drive a car we are perfectly capable of changing gear, keeping an eye on the road and other traffic, talking to a passenger, whilst also looking out for a petrol station. We do this by rationing the amount of attention that we pay to each of these actions, concentrating on that which is most important and less on everything else. Remember how tired you felt when you were learning to drive, because since nothing came automatically, you tried to concentrate on everything at once?

It is quite clear that selectivity of attention is an important factor in cricketing success and psychologists believe that it is a skill that can be learned. Since normal net practice provides few distractions, the coach needs to simulate, if possible, conditions in which the cricketer's attention is distracted. This might help the cricketer to develop selective attention.

*Alertness* refers to the sharpness of attention that the cricketer can display. His ability to maintain concentration at the end of a hot day at the crease is one example, as is that of the fielder who has had little to do and then, suddenly has the chance to make a difficult catch.

The sport psychologist is interested in *attentional styles,* which can be classified into those with a *broad* or *narrow* focus, and then further divided in to *internal* and *external*.[3] Attentional style is an important factor for the sportsman because not only is his attentional style critical to his performance, but it may even be critical to which sport he decides to pursue.

Let's look at these concepts in more detail.

## External or internal focus

The external focus refers to the attention paid to outward events such as the position of the fielders or the bowler's delivery. Internal focus refers to the cricketer's own thoughts and feelings – for example his strategy for the game, or how he plans to deal with a fast bowler. So you can imagine these two factors as being on a continuum from external objects 'out there', to an internal focus centred on the cricketer's own thought and feelings.

## Broad or narrow focus

When the focus is broad, the cricketer will be paying attention to several things at once – for example the position of fielders. When it is narrow, he is focusing on something more specific, for example the manner in which the bowler is delivering the ball.

From this we can see that there are four possible combinations of attention:

|  | Internal | External |
|---|---|---|
| **Broad** | Broad-internal e.g.planning tactics | Broad-external e.g.noting position of fielders |
| **Narrow** | Narrow-internal e.g. controlling anxiety Focus on effort, batting technique | Narrow-external e.g. watching the delivery of the ball |

**Figure 6** Model showing types of attentional focus

Robert Nideffer also introduced the concept of *information overload*[4] that refers to having too much information to absorb at any one time. Anyone who has started to use a computer for the first time will know what this feels like, having two or three manuals to skim as well as advice from well-meaning friends. In a cricket context one cannot help wondering what Alec Stewart must have felt like whilst England's captain, wicket keeper and opening bat.

Elsewhere, Robin Smith has said, "I wouldn't wish that on my worst enemy". As captain and opening bat his attentional focus would need to switch constantly from internal to external and from broad to narrow depending on whether he was thinking of tactics or the next delivery. He might also be aware of the reaction of the crowd, at the same time trying to ignore sledging from the slip fielders.

Nideffer also stated that increased arousal (see Chapter Five) will detract from our ability to pay attention. Most of us will have experienced at some time or other the inability to concentrate when we are anxious. In cricket, this can lead to a batsman paying insufficient attention to the position of the fielders; to him being distracted by the spectators; to a lack of judgement as to whether or not to leave the ball.

It is obvious that most sports will require the player to switch from one attentional style to another at varying times, but problems are likely to arise when a player relies too much on one style. For example, a narrow internal focus may lead to anxiety and the player worrying about the last innings in which he scored a duck rather than focusing on the events around him. A preoccupation with a broad external focus may lead the batsman to play indifferent strokes that are technically weak because he will be paying attention to what is 'out there' rather than to his technique.

Robert Nideffer has proposed that not only do sportspeople have different attentional styles but that they are either appropriate or inappropriate for the sport in which they are involved. He classified them as *effective attenders* or *ineffective attenders.*

Effective attenders are just that – they can switch from internal to external as required and from narrow focus to broad focus. This would enable them to deal appropriately with noisy spectators and with their own feelings of remorse if they had dropped a catch or had their partner run out. In this way they do not become overloaded with information. When England beat Zimbabwe in a one-day match in South Africa at the end of the 1999 – 2000 tour, Graeme Hick was run out whilst on 80. The Times reported that his partner, Darren Maddy, "continued as calmly as if the misunderstanding had never occurred", and completed his maiden half-century at Test level. It was clearly not a case of Maddy being unconcerned, but of him simply refusing to allow himself to be distracted.

Ineffective attenders are unable to concentrate at the required level. They may therefore be disturbed by the shouts of supporters or fail to notice changes in the fielding positions.

The importance to the coach of attentional focus is obvious. His task is to try to determine what the best attentional focus might be for each player, and if possible to deploy him accordingly – in other words help him to play to his attentional strengths rather than to any weakness.

Steve Oldham, Cricket Development Officer at Yorkshire CCC says that younger players find it more difficult to concentrate than do older players. "It's a problem when they go from playing schools cricket to men's cricket, the latter being longer. The Yorkshire Academy has some young players in the Yorkshire League, which is quite a good league, and we find they'll be OK for 15 – 20 overs, or if they are getting wickets, and then they nod off. They lose concentration and wander from position and the game seems to drift."

Any comments on concentration would not be complete without some reference to the practice of sledging – deliberate attempts to distract the batsman from his task. At Test level, this has become far more prevalent in recent years, with the Australian, Pakistani and South African teams making the most frequent use of this technique. Nor is this peculiar to cricket of course, since almost every sport seems to indulge in gamesmanship of one type or another. Sometimes, as with sledging the intention is simply to break the other competitor's concentration, as in this example quoted by Nideffer.

---

At a swim meet, two swimmers were standing on the starting blocks. The starter called them to their marks. One of the individuals intentionally false-started. He dived in, swam underwater into his opponent's lane, and then slowly swam back down the lane to the end of the pool. As he climbed out next to his competitor and walked past, he whispered, "I just pissed in your lane". The next time the starter called them to their marks, his competitor had difficulty directing attention to the starter's commands. As the gun went off, he got a slow start because he was thinking of diving into a puddle of urine instead of into the water.

---

What can the coach do to help players maintain their concentration? One technique that has been shown to work is for the coach to simulate a situation in which the player consistently loses concentration or has a decision go against him. He then learns to adjust his behaviour accordingly, and is therefore more likely to retain his concentration when the situation next occurs in a game rather than in practice.

If good concentration is likely to lead to plenty of runs, does poor concentration lead to disaster? Not necessarily! Former England Test player Robin Smith[5] quotes the example of Graham Gooch who kept his concentration while playing badly:

> *"It was in Gooch's 2nd innings against the New Zealanders in Auckland in 1992."  Smith wrote, "Graham scored 114, and he wasn't just bad, he was atrocious.  He was playing as poorly on 114 as he was on 0, yet it didn't bother him.  Goochie would either play and miss, or hit the ball for four.  There was no in-between, and poor Danny Morrison must have been tearing his hair out wondering what he had to do to get him out.  We were killing ourselves with laughter at Goochie's ineptitude, but it was a remarkable innings. Most batsmen would have given their wicket away at 20, assuming they had survived that long, but Graham was so mentally strong that he could forget about the bad shots and go on to notch up another Test century."*

But in spite of examples to the contrary for 'mere mortals', concentration needs to be developed.  Here are some ways of doing so:-

- For the batsman or bowler to remain positive, whatever the situation, they must lock themselves into the present.
- Concentrate on each delivery of the ball, not anticipating the next one, thinking about the last one, or the end of the over.
- Direct attention solely to the delivery of the ball, or the stroke to be played.  Concentrate on this and not on the result.  Results will come later!
- Don't be preoccupied with avoiding failure.  Think success.
- Don't give a second thought to unfair decisions or anything else over which you have no control.  You will

simply become frustrated and that is likely to have just one result.

- Practice focusing off the field as well as on it. One mental exercise, known as Chevreul's Pendulum, requires you to take a plumb bob, or any piece of string with a small weight attached to it. Steady your arm if necessary, but let the weight dangle in front of you. Visualise the weight moving in a circle. You will soon see that the weight will move in the same direction. You are sending very slight impulses down your arm, which are then reflected in the rotation of the weight. With practice, you will be able to move it clockwise or anti-clockwise.

# CHECK LIST FOR ATTENTIONAL FOCUS AND STYLE

❖ The ability to concentrate is critical to sporting success.

❖ It is physically impossible to concentrate 100% indefinitely and therefore batsmen and bowlers need to develop a technique in which they can alternate between concentration and temporary relaxation.

❖ *Selectivity* refers to the ability to focus attention on one specific issue at a particular moment.

❖ Alertness *refers to the sharpness of attention paid; to awareness and readiness.*

❖ Attentional styles can be external or internal, and focused broadly or narrowly.

❖ External broad, for example, might refer to the position of the fielders, and external narrow might refer to the bowler's delivery.

❖ Internal broad might refer to the planning and tactics of the game, whilst internal narrow, would indicate a concentration on one's own feelings, anxiety, or effort exerted.

❖ The brain is able to filter out that which does not directly help us to achieve our goal.

❖ *Information overload* refers to a situation in which we are expected to absorb more than we can take in over a short period.

❖ Encourage players to develop their concentration in the nets and also off the field.

# 9    Confidence, self esteem and self efficacy

*His record, taken all in all,*
*Was not a very great one;*
*He seldom hit a crooked ball*
*And never stopped a straight one.*

*The Rabbit*
Anon

At the first of the Bradford Cricket Management and Coaching Skills courses, each coach was asked to complete a personality questionnaire, the purpose of which was to provide him with an insight into his own strengths and areas for development. (See Chapter 14 The Personality of the Coach for details.)

The results were fascinating.

## Confidence

The collective profile of the coaches and would-be coaches showed that as a group, they were somewhat lacking in confidence. On a 10 point scale they scored 6 (10 showing extreme self doubt, and 1 extreme confidence.) They were all well-experienced and had played cricket at first class county level – some even at Test Match level – for many years. How was it, that those who could play cricket in front of several thousand spectators, players whose names were well known in the sporting world, some of whom even enjoyed star status, could show anything other than a high level of confidence? Shouldn't they have high self-esteem?

## Self-esteem

It is a strange fact that the majority of us develop negative and self-critical attitudes early in life, seldom missing an opportunity to put ourselves down. To do otherwise, to praise ourselves and give ourselves deserved credit, is thought to be conceited, or self-satisfied, certainly within our British culture. We do not like those who boast, even if it is justified.

As stated elsewhere, American studies have shown that over 60% of the population have low self-esteem, and this figure includes many people who would generally be classed as successful in the sense that they have good jobs, are intelligent, dress well, etc. Why should this be? Self-esteem is something of a plastic quality that is largely shaped in childhood, and is reasonably firm around the age of 11 or 12 years old. It can, however be improved in later life, and the cricket coach should be aware of this.

Low self-esteem is thought to be largely a result of how we have interacted with our parents and other authority figures, in which the emphasis is usually on negative statements. "Don't do that," or "You ought to try harder," or "You could have done better than that." Usually, as coaches, bosses, parents, we are so concerned with correcting what we believe to be negative, that we forget to comment on the positive. "Catch people doing something right," said Ken Blanchard in the One-Minute Manager.

How often have we been in meetings and thought of an idea, but not mentioned it, only to have someone else come up with the idea later – and receive credit for it. It is the fear of rejection that prevents us from saying something at the right time – the fear of a 'put down' such as, "What makes you think that's such a great idea?" or, "That's ridiculous." This fear of rejection seems to pervade much of what we say and do. In sport it might prevent someone from setting himself goals. Why? Because if you don't set them, you can't not achieve them! Sales people might not make that daunting telephone call for fear of rejection. What if they say No? It is this fear of failure, and of rejection, that prevents us from taking a bolder view of life.

If a player is criticised, he might shrug it off, but if his self-esteem is low - if he has self-doubt - he might take it too much to heart. Let's take a practical example. If a coach calls an obviously intelligent player stupid, the player is unlikely to take the comment seriously, because in his heart, he knows he is not stupid. He can point to diplomas or degrees to prove it, if he was so minded. So although he may not relish the comment, he does not let it worry him. His self-esteem is unlikely to be damaged, because he has ample evidence that he is intelligent. If the coach tells him disparagingly that his batting is mediocre, and the player has self-doubt in this regard, then his self-esteem might become even lower. This is likely to impede any improvement in his batting technique.

We need to reverse this pattern. We need to remind ourselves of our successes, which we tend to take for granted, thinking perhaps, that everyone else has had similar successes. The cricket coach can encourage players to think of the successes that they have had, to dwell on the things they do well, instead of concentrating solely on 'areas for improvement.' The latter are important – but not at the expense of blotting out entirely the positive characteristics and abilities that we might have. As children, we are taught humility, but it is a false humility. If we have a talent it can be stated simply as a matter of fact. It is no different than saying we are five-foot ten inches tall, or that we have blue eyes. Players need to remind themselves regularly of their attributes and the coach should encourage them to do this.

## Self efficacy

Let's return to the comment made at the beginning of this chapter, to the effect that many cricketers had low or average levels of confidence in spite of their obvious successes on the field. Why should this be so?

The answer to this question has received much attention from sport psychologists in recent years. What the personality profile showed, was confidence as a global personality trait. In other words it described the amount of confidence that players might show in their normal everyday lives. Sport psychologists have identified a particular aspect of self-confidence, known as *self-efficacy*, and it is the strength of *this* factor that indicates the degree of confidence that the sportsman might have, in succeeding at a specific task.

John Emburey demonstrated this when, drawing on his vast experience at Test and county level, he said:

> *"I was always confident in what I did as a spin bowler. I had good control over length and line. I wasn't a big spinner of the ball, but because I had good change of pace and flight, I knew what I was trying to do. I could bowl to a field that was set for me, and I knew I could always bowl economically in Test cricket, but I also knew that if the wicket turned, I had the ability to get wickets as well."*

All sportsmen are aware that confidence is an essential ingredient to success. Relating this to teams, as well as to individuals, Morris and

Summers[1] Australian sports psychologists, quote the example of the England v Australia Test Match in 1993. They say:

*"Australia certainly had a better balanced team and it was probably more skilful, man for man, but the stranglehold which permitted Australia to turn around the few difficult situations they met illustrates the difference in confidence between the teams that summer. When they found themselves under pressure, Australia did not think about defeat and they pulled things around, while England did not believe they could win, so they let their chances slip."*

Self-efficacy is a concept derived from general psychology and has been explored in the context of sport by Albert Bandura[2] and others. He defines self-efficacy as the belief a person might have in his capability to perform a specific task. He describes it as essentially a thinking process. Psychologists call this a *cognitive* process. It is a subjective judgement, reflecting what the person believes he can do. It does not necessarily relate to what he *can* do. Therefore a cricketer might have a high degree of self-efficacy, although his actual performance level may not warrant it. Conversely, he might have a high level of skill, but if his self-efficacy is low, he is less likely to perform well. Usually however, self-efficacy and level of skill are about the same. This is due to one key influence – *that of his past performances.* Therefore a bowler who has taken several wickets at the expense of only a few runs, is likely to have high self-efficacy when he comes to bowl the next over. The reason is that his self-efficacy – his belief that he can successfully perform the specific task of bowling – will be based on the most powerful indicator of all – his immediate past performance.

Listen to Jack Birkenshaw, now a talent scout for the ECB as well as Head Coach at Leicestershire CCC.

*"Confidence is such a massive ingredient towards success. I've seen some of the best players in the world when they're lacking in confidence. Their movements are less sharp. It doesn't matter how great a player you are, even the best lose confidence after several failures. You think today's going to be a great day, and it's not. After you get four or five ducks on the trot you begin to*

> *doubt. It doesn't matter how much people might*
> *encourage you, when you walk out to the middle with*
> *four or five ducks behind you, you wonder where the*
> *next run's coming from. I saw Greg Chappell get about*
> *six or seven noughts in Australia against the West Indies.*
> *He must have doubted whether he was ever going to get*
> *a run again. At one stage in his career he was always*
> *confident. But then a run of bad scores, and even the*
> *toughest competitor is affected".*

He went on to say that before a game he would talk to a player, perhaps reminding him of his successes, playing videos, and trying to bolster his confidence. *"But when he's out in the middle he's on his own. It's eleven players against one. If he has a good defence, that can help because he will be able to make time to play himself in. If he can survive for half an hour, gradually his confidence will get stronger."*

There is of course, an obvious link here with motivation. Researchers claim that the level of self-efficacy that a player has will be related to his choice of sport, or a particular aspect of that sport. So for example, if a player has high self-efficacy as a fielder and only moderate self-efficacy as a batsman, he is likely to prefer fielding to batting. This is his choice. It follows that he will be more strongly motivated to field rather than bat. There is also a clear relationship here, with effort and persistence. If a player has high self-efficacy in one aspect of his sport, he is likely to put in the required effort to be successful. He is also likely to be more persistent, and will be more determined to overcome difficulties. These three factors – choice of activity, effort, and persistence – are elements of motivation.

The young Lancashire cricketer, Andy Flintoff, who had a meteoric rise from being a rather casual, amateur player to being picked for inclusion in England's World Cup team, and later for the winter tour of South Africa, had this to say about confidence: *"I try to respect bowlers but when I'm batting I need to be confident and feel like I'm playing for St. Anne's again. That's where I learned to hit it straight because there is a short straight boundary there."*

According to Bruce Grobbbelaar, the former Liverpool FC goalkeeper, his successor at Anfield should have been David James, and that James should have been in contention with Arsenal's David Seaman for the England goalkeeping position. He believes that James had the attributes to be one of the best in the world, but that, *"James had to get his head right and believe in himself. Nobody at Liverpool ever got into his mind, nobody ever worked him out."* Bob Wilson, Seaman's coach at Arsenal, endorses that comment. "I remember going to Liverpool and watching David James with their goalkeeping coach Joe Corrigan. What came through was that Joe could not make him believe how good he was, yet he had everything a goalkeeper needs."

Graeme Hick has been equally puzzling. On his day, he can be as mighty as Lance Klusener, just as powerful and twice as elegant, and Duncan Fletcher's task is to get him to realise it, said the Daily Mail. The difference is that Klusener has always risen to the occasion and Hick hasn't. It seems that his confidence is variable, yet here is a cricketer who has had a glittering career by any standards, a man who made his first century for his school team at the age of six; at 17 he was the youngest player in the Prudential World Cup; the youngest player ever to represent Zimbabwe; the youngest player ever to score 2,000 runs in an English season; one of Wisden's Five Cricketer's of the Year in 1986; the youngest batsman ever to score 50 first-class centuries; a man who scored 405 runs for Worcester against Somerset (the highest individual score in England since 1895); top of the first-class batting averages in 1997. The accolades could go on. Yet in the South Africa tour of 1999 – 2000 he scored just 50 in his first five innings. In the face of so much previous success, how can confidence be so mercurial?

On the morning that the great Basil D'Oliveira was due to play his famous innings at The Oval – the fifth Test against Australia in 1968 – he telephoned his wife. He said, *"Get the neighbours to look after the kids and pull up a chair in front of the television. I'm going to bat all day."* He scored 158.

We have seen that self-efficacy is an important aspect of sporting performance, and therefore a subject that demands the close attention of the coach who will be concerned to raise the self-efficacy of those under his care. Confidence and self-efficacy feed each other: sporting success should increase general confidence to some extent and the level of self-efficacy at a particular task; high self-efficacy ("you know you can do it because you've done it"), is likely to generate the self-efficacy necessary for the next performance. So how does the coach raise the level of self-efficacy? There are four areas to which he needs to turn his attention.

First, as just mentioned, is the actual *previous performance* of the player. This is the most powerful indicator of future performance.

("Why look into the crystal ball, when you can read the book?" said a former politician.) For the same reason, a previous failure may encourage a player to think negatively about the approaching task. "I failed last time. I'll probably fail this time." Other factors are also relevant. What about the difficulty of the task? If the player has succeeded at something regarded as difficult, his self-efficacy will be higher than if he had succeeded at a relatively easy task. In addition, did he succeed on his own, or was it a team effort? If it was an individual effort, his self-efficacy will be higher than if the result depended on others.

The coach needs to consider performance accomplishment in the light of what is realistic and appropriate for a particular player. Performance targets need to be challenging but attainable, otherwise there may be little increase in self-efficacy.

Second, the successful performance of another player can heighten self-efficacy. If a player has skills roughly equal to another's, and he performs well against that other player, it is likely to have the effect of raising self-efficacy. "If he can do it, I can do it," might be an appropriate comment. This is known as *vicarious experience*.

Third, the coach may well tell the player that he can succeed at a particular task, but this will only work when the coach is recognised as being honest as well as knowledgeable and competent in the eyes of the player, and when such encouragement is given sparingly. Used too frequently it will become meaningless in the eyes of the player, and worse, the credibility of the coach will be diminished.

Imagery can also be used effectively to boost levels of confidence. Note the comments of Michael Atherton and Jack Nicklaus in the chapter on Mental Rehearsal.

Finally, and a further aspect of Bandura's theory, is that of repeated success through *participatory modelling*. Here, the player sees the 'model' perform a task and then successfully performs it himself with help from the model. The theory is that with repeated success the player's level of self-efficacy will rise. However, in my experience of judo, top class performers do not always realise that what they do in competition can be very different from what they are able to demonstrate, breaking down an action into constituent parts. A world-class Japanese light heavyweight was demonstrating his favourite throw to a group of judo players but was, in fact, doing something quite different from that which he had used to such devastating affect in competition!

## Self-talk

Self-talk, and affirmations – another technique for raising self-esteem – are usually dealt with only briefly in sport psychology books, and therefore this longer account might be useful to the cricket coach as well as the general reader.

Many sportspeople find the concept of self-talk to be helpful. This simply involves making and repeating positive statements to ourselves. If you think that sort of behaviour to be odd, just consider your own habits for a moment. I am sure that you will be obliged to agree that you engage in a continuous stream of self-talk – internal thought processing, if you prefer. If the player's thoughts are realistic, he is likely to function well. But if they are negative, exaggerated, or irrational, his emotions are affected and his performance is likely to suffer also. *Positive* self-talk can help you to direct your thoughts in a more productive and manner. We have seen in Chapter Five, that fear or anxiety are simply labels that we attach to certain events which affect us negatively, but may not affect someone else similarly. We need to switch our thinking from the negative to the positive. If for example a batsman is nervous awaiting his innings, he can either think: "I am so uptight, my heart is pounding, I'm sweating, my stomach is churning, I know I'm not going to do well," or he can believe that because of these physical symptoms, his body is attuned to the task before him, and this can just as easily be interpreted as "I'm keyed up to produce an excellent performance; I'm alert, focused on what I have to do, and I'm ready to go out there and win." Same physical symptoms, just a positive way of interpreting them.

Muhammad Ali's *"I am the greatest,"* is probably the most memorable piece of self-talk any of us is ever likely to hear.

What do cricketers say to themselves when they are playing? Do their thoughts help them to play better? Are their thoughts likely to be positive, thereby adding to their confidence, or negative, lowering their self-efficacy? Unless they have made a deliberate attempt to encourage a positive attitude within themselves, the chances are that their thoughts will be negative. We are all the product of our thoughts. So it's an almost certain bet that the cricket coach will find that many of his players have negative thoughts, in spite of the fact that most will be aware of the value of having the right mental attitude in sport.

What usually happens is that we carry on negative self-talk at a sub-vocal level. "I'm not good enough for the team," "I am a weak link in an otherwise good team," "I hope I don't fail again today," " I hope I don't let the side down." "What if I drop an important catch?" Most people have a tendency to think in this negative manner, rather than to say, "I'm going out there to win," "I shall do my best to make this my best innings of the season." Psychologists say we can have as many as 50,000 thought in a day – up to 5,000 thoughts an hour, and if the majority of those are negative, we can begin to understand why so many have low self-esteem.

As a coach you might like to select one or two players whom you think might lack self-confidence and encourage them to change their negative thoughts into positive ones. For every negative thought, they need to produce one or two positive statements. Ask them to think of situations in which they tend to be negative and then ask them to replace their negative thoughts with one or two which are positive. Tell them to write them down.

| Negative statements | Positive statements |
|---|---|
| 1.  I've never batted well against this bowler. | 1.  I'm going to get 50 runs today. |
| 2.  Another dropped catch and I might be out of the team. | 2.  I'm feeling really good today - loose, nimble and alert. |
| 3.  This net practice is boring. | 3.  I'm going to stick with it and improve my batting. |

Emphasise the power of positive statements expressed as "I am..." sentences. When we think negatively, we behave negatively. Invite your players to think of the benefits that can flow from positive statements.

## Affirmations

The idea behind affirmations is that we become what we believe ourselves to be. An affirmation is the writing down of clear statements of an outcome that you wish to achieve. To be effective these need to be stated in positive terms, such as "I am happily looking at the trophy I have won this season." It needs to be in the present tense, brief, specific, and contain an active verb. It should also relate to your feelings at the time of the action – 'happily', 'gladly', etc. These affirmations need to be repeated several times a day. They can be written down on index cards – the very act of writing them down is beneficial. The player can close his eyes and visualise the result, seeing it in full colour if possible. If he imagines a positive event he will motivate himself. Remember that the mind cannot tell the difference between a real event and an imagined event. The experiment you conducted in which you imagined yourself at the top of a tall building looking down on a street hundreds of feet below, was proof of this.

The brain's reticular system is a network of neural circuits. This system plays an important role not only in controlling our state of arousal, but also in our ability to focus attention on one specific stimulus. The system appears to act as a filter allowing some sensory messages to get through to our conscious awareness while blocking out others. Feel what is going on in your feet. You are suddenly aware of them, yet nothing has changed. The feeling in your feet is the same now as it was before, but you are now aware of that feeling.

The reticular system seems to let in anything that allows us to achieve our goal. If we learn a new word, we soon see it in print. When we need petrol for the car we soon see filling stations. So when we have a goal, we begin to see things that will enable us to achieve that goal, the reticular system allowing us to see things that match our self-image, and filter out things that do not. In this way, the affirmations that we write down, and which we repeat regularly, become part of our self-image, and we have enhanced our chances of success.

# CHECK LIST FOR SELF-EFFICACY

❖ Confidence is a personality characteristic. Because it is a general statement about confidence in a variety of situations, it is a global characteristic.

❖ Psychologists have identified a component of global confidence known as self-efficacy. This refers to a display of confidence in a specific situation, e.g. playing cricket.

❖ A powerful booster of self-efficacy is the knowledge of one's previous successful performances. Past performance is the best predictor of future performance. An over-awareness of previous failures will lower self-efficacy and self-esteem generally.

❖ Success and failure need to be regarded as relative terms. An improvement of performance against realistic goals is a success, and should enhance self-efficacy.

❖ The success of another player can help to improve an individual performance, particularly if both players have roughly equal ability. "If he can do it, I can do it." This is known as vicarious experience.

❖ Sincere encouragement from the coach will help to raise self-efficacy, providing it is used sparingly.

❖ Imagery is a useful aid to raising self-efficacy.

❖ Participatory modelling refers to the player's modelling himself on the successful performance of a technique by another player. With repeated success, the player's self-efficacy will rise.

❖ Self-talk refers to positive statements designed to counter the negative thinking common to many of us. They should be expressed in the present tense and repeated regularly. The cricket coach can encourage players to develop positive mental attitudes in this way.

❖ Affirmations are brief written statements of an outcome that the player wishes to achieve. As with self-talk, they need to be positive statements, containing an active verb. They should be read several times a day.

❖ The brain's reticular system filters out sensory messages that do not help us achieve our goal, and allows through, those messages that are significant to us. When we have a goal, written down in the form of an affirmation, the brain will help us to see things likely to aid our achievement of that goal.

# 10  Oral communication

> *"Our matches began at 2.30 and as usual on that*
> *Saturday afternoon I threw my bag into the car about*
> *half-past one to be in good time.  But I had reckoned*
> *without the Russians. 'You must come back, you're*
> *wanted very urgently on the phone,' [said a child.]  My*
> *leisurely contemplation of the afternoon's game was*
> *shattered.  In fact I was urgently wanted on two*
> *telephones.  We had two different lines, one the normal*
> *house phone and the other an extension from the Jodrell*
> *[Bank] switchboard.  The telephones had rung in*
> *chorus.  The duty controller from Jodrell conveyed a*
> *business-like message that the Russians had 'launched a*
> *rocket that would reach the moon on Sunday evening'.*
> *The voice on the house phone was that of an excited*
> *pressman asking what we were going to do about it.  My*
> *answer was brief: 'I am going to play cricket.'*

> *The Moon Match*
> Sir Bernard Lovell

Pick up almost any book on sports coaching, almost any book on management, and almost any book dealing with a human activity, and you will read about the importance of communication. Such books are usually long on the need to be able to communicate with all and sundry, and short on how to do it effectively.

Ask anyone who works in an organisation of any reasonable size if they can suggest improvements in the way the unit is managed, and they will almost invariably say that communication could be improved.

To which one could reply: "Of course it could!"

Even in large organisations who employ a 'communications officer', it may well be the case that communications are not perfect. Can they ever be?  Are we not baying for the moon to expect that communications will be perfect in any organisation that is active, dynamic, and which needs to respond to external pressures, be they sport spectators, the media, or ordinary 'customers'?  Perhaps so, but the ability to communicate clearly and acceptably is fundamental to coaching.

In this chapter we are dealing with several aspects of communication.

First there is communication that is essential to the smooth running of your club. This can be summed up in the need to let all members know what is happening, where and when. There are of course the ordinary day to day issues, but in addition, people will want to know where the organisation is heading. What are the key issues for now and the immediate future, and how are they to be tackled? Although some of these matters may lie more within the responsibility of the club committee, the coach should also play his part in disseminating and explaining the club's policies and objectives.

The coach's main responsibility as a communicator will be with each player; in team talks; and in making presentations to the chief executive of the club committee.

## One-to-one communication

It may well be that in the future, communication between a cricket coach and his players will be transformed. In the 1999 World Cup, South African captain Hansie Cronje and the fast bowler Allan Donald, took to the field with tiny radios in their right ears, linking them to the voice of Bob Woolmer, their respected coach. The innovation was immediately banned, but the International Cricket Council has said that they will need to discuss the matter. After all, runs the argument, is it any different from a football coach shouting from the touchline? One of the South African batsmen was so keen on the benefits of being coached while at the crease, that he ordered his own radio, to be worn beneath the helmet. Apparently earpieces cost about £800 each; the coach's apparatus, a headset, about £5,000. Bob Woolmer commented that his innovation would take the game forward and speed it up, and added that for decades, coaches and captains have been sending out instructions on the pretext of delivering a fresh set of batting gloves! (This topic was discussed at a cricket coach's course at Bradford University – see Appendix 3 for a summary of key points.)

Carling and Heller[1] point out that the outstanding coach of the post war years has been Frank Dick whose skills as a communicator (and therefore motivator) had a tremendous impact on British athletics. Middle-distance running, sprinting, and javelin throwing personified by Coe, Cram and Ovett; Christie and Regis; Whitbread and Backley - all benefited from his gifts as a communicator and therefore as a coach. As further testament to his ability, note that Dick did not confine himself to athletics: he also worked with Boris Becker and racing driver Gerhard Berger. His coaching and development philosophy was summed up in the phrase *"the only two gifts you can give [your pupils] are the roots to grow and the wings to fly."* He extended that to hold good not just for coaches and their sportsmen, but teachers and pupils, and managers and their staff.

Frank Dick demonstrated another characteristic of importance to the coach: that of building on strengths instead of concentrating on weaknesses. Whilst coaching Berger, he had the task of trying to increase the driver's endurance, and would normally have recommended running. However Berger hated running but fortunately loved squash, which served the purpose adequately. The point here, is that coaches need to think laterally, to be prepared to follow a different path if that is what the situation calls for. Too often we repeat the tired and stale solutions prevalent at the time of our own development, and stick with those ideas. Cricket, like any other sport, needs to develop, but will whither if its adherents resist change.

Frank Dick's approach to coaching is worthy of comment. At the initial stage, his attitude towards an athlete would be directive. The athlete was told what he had to do, and when he had to do it. Because the athlete realised that acquiring a coach was a significant step in his career, he responded to this approach. In other words, his motivation was high. His performances would then improve but not as fast as he had hoped, and therefore his motivation decreased. At this stage the coach would change from a directive style to a 'coaching' style, which was a little softer, and allowed the athlete more latitude. At both of these stages, the coach was still in control. At stage three, the athlete realised that he was on the right track. He had ambitions and saw that he was capable of realising them. At the fourth stage, the coach relinquished control, but made it clear that he supported what the athlete was doing. At the final stage, both motivation and confidence were high, and at that stage the coach's role is simply to be there for when he is needed.

The first two stages provided the roots and the second two the wings.

## Small group communication

Here it is important that the group is small enough for the coach to be able to communicate face-to-face with each person. The coach's communication job is to ensure that there is free discussion between him and the group so that ideas and strategies can be aired without losing sight of the ultimate goal – to be able to improve team and individual performances.

To do this, the coach needs to understand his players. Since cricket has a strong social side to it, the coach will probably know his players fairly well, but it may still be helpful if he thinks about the strengths and weaknesses of each player, and addresses his comments accordingly. If necessary refresh your memory of Chapter One and refer to Appendix 2 showing Belbin's Nine Team Role Types. A perceptive coach should be able to make a fair guess as to what each player might be able to contribute by looking at both the positive and negative qualities in Belbin.

There are of course a few techniques that the coach should employ in order to be a successful communicator:

- Prepare what you are going to say. Even three or four words jotted down hurriedly may be sufficient to prevent you from overlooking an important point. What is your objective? What style is most likely to be productive – are you going to 'tell and sell', ask, listen, or problem solve? Each style has advantages and disadvantages. Your style of communication will depend on what it is you wish to achieve.
- Talk clearly.
- Try to modulate your voice. It needs pace and pitch. Even a five-minute talk can seem an eternity to the listener if the speaker drones on in a monotone. If the group is dying on you, do not be afraid to raise your voice. Dropping the voice to a stage whisper also can be effective. Attention improves.
- Any criticism should be constructive. In other words, the coach needs to emphasise what the player should do to correct a fault, rather than concentrate on what has been done incorrectly.
- A useful guideline is to try to make two positive comments before you make a negative one (or one that the player

may regard as negative). Like any other technique however, this will be predictable if it is used too often.

- Give encouragement always, and give praise when it is deserved. The currency of praise will be debased if it is used too often; if used rarely, it may be insufficient to ward off the development of a player's negative attitude.
- Never, never, use sarcasm.
- Remember that cricket is a game to be enjoyed. Gleeson[2] emphasises enjoyment as an important part of the learning process. The Cricket Coach's Manual, published by the England and Wales Cricket Board contains a number of suggestions for cricket games, and of course the coach can use his own imagination to devise games which contain an element of skill relevant to some aspect of cricket.
- Always use words that are appropriate for the age group you are coaching.
- Ensure that you have sufficient material to make the coaching session worthwhile – but not so much that players will have difficulty in retaining it all.

## Team meetings

Australian Test cricketer Steve Waugh says *"It is every captain's dream to have each player know their game plan – being confident and positive in what they do, exploiting their strengths and minimising their weaknesses."* Writing in the Sunday Times, he had some insightful comments to make about his teammate Michael Bevan:

> *"In team meetings he is generally a listener, taking it all in until he thinks he can make a contribution, which invariably is spot on, and is observed by others with great interest. One of Bev's most thought provoking lines came when he said: "Fielding is a true test of one's character because it is the only thing in which you truly commit yourself to the team and which you do not get statistically rewarded for."*

Clive Rice, former captain and now coach of Nottinghamshire County Cricket Club, emphasises the need for the coach to invite comment from the team. *"Some players can contribute fantastically,"* he said. *"Even if you win a game, you have to discuss what went wrong, because there's bound to be something. I like to leave things for two days before analysing team performances. You've got to wait for the adrenalin to die down."*

Perhaps one of the most difficult things for a coach or captain to do in connection with team talks is to keep it fresh. Eventually, situations will repeat themselves and new ways may need to be found to put across an old message. Long serving football managers and coaches in particular have this problem. Few people will forget the extraordinary climax to the 1999 European Cup Final between Manchester United and Bayern Munich in Barcelona at which United were losing 1 – 0 until the last 3 minutes of extra time when United scored twice to win the European Championship, and of course, the Treble. For much of the time United had not played to their usual high standard. So what did their manager, Alex Ferguson say to them at half time? Just 24 words, apparently.

*"The cup will only be six feet away from you at the end of this night. If you lose, you can't even touch it."* He added, *"Do not come back in here without giving your all."* Later, he said this about team talks: *"I had the message in my mind and I knew what I wanted to say to them. You have to find a way to affect people's lives. One obvious way is through motivation, but there are different ways of doing it. Sometimes you can ruin the whole effect. It isn't easy. If you just* look *at some players they melt before your gaze. Sometimes I have gone over the top at half-time or at the end of games. But then, they have known how much it means to me. Eventually it seeps into their pores and you hope, in the end they are like that themselves. Some of them will become managers and they will have to have the ability to get through to everyone. That becomes a characteristic of your team. My 1994 Double-winning team had mental toughness. So many of them were tough b\*\*\*\*\*\*s. I said this present bunch could only be judged on what they could achieve. Now they are the best, they are legends."*

## General points to be observed

The following points are largely common sense and can be found in one form or another in coaching textbooks. Most coaches will be aware of these points, but they are offered here as a mental refresher, and to see them written will be helpful in this regard.

- The player must have a clear understanding of the essential movement required in a cricketing skill.
- The correct action must be demonstrated. The first demonstration of a technique is likely to make a lasting impression on the player. One failing is to demonstrate a technique slowly so that everyone can see it. However, in most sports, a technique demonstrated slowly is not the same as one performed at normal speed. The slow demonstration, if thought necessary, should be carried out *after* the one at normal speed.
- If a demonstration of a cricketing technique is not as good as was intended, the correct method should be demonstrated several times, so that these will be the impressions left in the player's mind.
- Ensure that the pace of the coaching session is right. Is the group looking confused? (Slow down and explain more clearly what is required.) Is it looking bored? (Speed up. It could be that you are talking too much, and turning the coaching session into a speech! Remember they have come to acquire cricketing skills.)
- Do not finish a coaching session with a demonstration leaving the group with no opportunity to practice it. This will simply make them frustrated.
- A member of the group can be chosen to demonstrate a technique if the coach is confident of his ability to do so. This will not only boost the confidence of the player chosen but of the rest of the group also. The thought that "If he can do it, I can," would be a most satisfactory outcome.
- Remember that the demonstration should be carried out in the same manner, as it would be in a match.

## Communication with management

Without doubt the key to a successful presentation for most of us is that of preparation. Only a very few, a talented minority, can make an effective presentation with little or no preparation.

The first consideration is to determine your audience. This is important because you will need to pitch your presentation at the right level. You will need to ask yourself how much the audience already knows about your subject. Technical words – jargon perhaps – are best avoided, but if you feel it is justified, are you sure that each member of the audience will understand? How much does the audience know about your subject?

The cricket coach should be in a strong position in as much as he will know members of the committee, he will know the club secretary or the chief executive. This means he will be familiar with their preferences and how they are likely to react to a presentation. Do they like detail or do they prefer the big picture? How important will they regard any financial aspects of your proposal? Do they like to think strategically? You will be in a stronger position and much more likely to succeed if you have give these matters some thought as you prepare your presentation.

Second, you need to be clear in your own mind about the purpose of your presentation. What are you trying to do? Is it to persuade someone to adopt a particular course of action? Is it to explain your strategy for the coming season? Is it a straight 'tell and sell' session, or are you looking for ideas and suggestions from your audience? In order to be clear about your objective you need to continually ask yourself "why?" Make sure that you have one clear objective. Then, when you are clear about your objective, you can begin to shape what you are going to say.

As a coach it is important that you select the right audience. In first class county cricket, you may need to talk to the company secretary, or the chief executive. It may be that your request can only be dealt with by the cricket committee, so it is important that you know clearly who has the authority to accede to your request or sanction your course of action. At amateur cricket level there will no doubt be a similar cricket committee or club secretary. Do not waste the time of people who may only be able to refer your query elsewhere.

Your third consideration will be to tailor your talk to the amount of time available. This is probably the most difficult thing to do, and the solution is probably the most contentious! We all love talking about a topic with which we are familiar, but brevity is the key to a successful presentation. We are not talking about a lecture, but the ability to put your point across concisely, and perhaps to an audience who would rather be doing something else. Consider the following statements:

*"He just goes on and on."*

*"He talked for over half an hour, and I still don't know
what he was going on about."*

*"If only he'd get to the point."*

*"He wants to see me for twenty minutes.   That means an
hour unless I cut him off."*

We have all made comments similar to this, but in turn, most of us have also been the culprit when it has been our turn to address a group.  It is possible to make our point in a very short time span – some advocate a maximum of one minute or even 30 seconds. That does not mean of course that the total meeting would be that length of time, but it does mean that after you have introduced your subject and prepared the ground in the manner you feel is appropriate, you can make the essence of your talk – *what you are there for* – in a very short period. Impossible?   Let's think for a moment how commercials and television reports are made. We know that most people have a very short attention span. Advertising researchers have found that our attention span is 30 seconds. What would our reaction be to a commercial that went on for five minutes? And yet if the brief 30-second commercial did not work, would organisations spend millions of pounds in television advertising? Of course not. At what point would our attention begin to wonder? Have you ever wondered why the vast majority of news reports are in fact little more than snippets? The average length of a television news story is 90 seconds. The story is introduced in the first 30 seconds, the 'guts' of the story takes another 30 seconds, and the reporter or news anchorman will sum up the story in the last 30 seconds. Back in the studio, the essential 30 seconds of the interview – the kernel of it, if you like – will be edited into a sound bite. Politicians of all parties are well practised in the technique of ensuring that their speeches contain a 'sound bite' element.. You can easily test these points for yourself: just look at the second hand of your watch when you next switch on your television set.  Even the big stories can all be split down into sub stories or different angles on the same event, so that we have a 30-second account from an eye witness, a short piece from a police officer, another perhaps from a psychologist.  What we do *not* have is a long piece from one person.

Now that you are clear in your own mind about the purpose of the presentation, you need to consider the best way in which to present it.

**Computer technology** has enabled us to produce professional presentations. If your club has a computer and Microsoft Office PowerPoint or a similar software package, you will be able to produce a presentation with maximum visual impact.

**OHP transparencies** have the advantage of acting as a kind of prompt for the material that you wish to cover. This is ideal for those who only make infrequent presentations. Each overhead projector transparency should be clear, carrying only a few key points. Use different colours for emphasis.

**Flip Charts** can enable you to present your material at minimum cost. Prepare each sheet well in advance and make sure that you writing is clear and easily legible from the back of the room.

# CHECK LIST FOR ORAL COMMUNICATION

The ability to communicate clearly is fundamental to good coaching.

Communication is defined here in its broadest sense – to include coverage of club issues, objectives and future plans, as well as more personal matters. It also includes coaching style.

Coaching styles (and therefore communication) need to be adapted according to the experience and seniority of the player.

❖ To be an effective communicator on a one-to-one basis the coach needs to understand the player and shape his message accordingly. The appendices showing Belbin team Role Types may be of use here.

❖ Preparation for team talks is essential.

❖ Post-match talks are best postponed for 24 or 48 hours whether the team has won or not. This allows time for more effective views to surface.

❖ Team talks need to be kept fresh if they are to have impact.

❖ Be mindful of basic coaching techniques – be clear about what you want to convey; ensure that demonstrations of technique are correct; control the pace of the coaching session.

❖ In presenting to a management group shape the presentation to the audience. Consider the balance between key points and detail.

❖ What is the purpose of your presentation? What do you want to achieve as an outcome?

❖ Time your talk. Don't waste people's time. Keep it as short as possible.

❖ Use technology to help you put your message across. Computerised presentation packages can be impressive, but so can well-presented OHP transparencies. Even the humble flip chart can be effective.

# 11 Active listening

*He will remember how he held a catch,*
*Or how he stayed two hours at the crease,*
*And by his stubborn effort saved the match*
*When none but he could still defend their wicket*
*Against such bowlers.  Dreaming thus of cricket,*
*While the fire crackles, he will be at peace.*

*An Old Man Dreams*
Anon

At first glance, it may seem obvious that a coach – indeed all of us – need to pay close attention to what others are saying. Listening is such a commonplace activity, that it hardly seems worthwhile to point out the advantages of careful listening.  But in this context, we are not talking simply about listening.  We are talking about *active listening,* something which few of us do conscientiously. What many of us do is to *hear*, which is not the same as to listen actively.

Most of us have never really learned to listen, yet this skill is basic to fruitful conversations with friends, at business meetings, during interviews, at conferences, in general discussion, and of course in coaching. Listening is a vital skill for a coach.  Indeed it is difficult to imagine how a coach can be fully effective unless he is a good listener.

As you develop your listening skills you will find that your understanding of others deepens; the more you become recognised as a good listener, the more likely it is that your players will confide in you and seek your advice.

Active listening involves several skills that have a twofold effect: that of encouraging the speaker to reveal more of his thoughts and concerns, and increasing the proportion of his speech that you positively hear.

Let us examine the reasons why we do not always listen to others as carefully as we might.

First, we tend to be selective in what we hear.  We 'tune out' those things that we believe are less important.  This applies not only to listening but also to everything else that goes on around us all the time. Thousands of messages or signals are received by our nervous system every minute. It is impossible to pay attention to all of them at the same time. Are you aware of any traffic outside? Now that I have brought this to your attention, you are possibly alert to the passing car or a distant motorcycle. We tend to concentrate on those things that we deem to be important at a particular moment. When we apply this principle to our listening abilities, we realise that we frequently 'tune out' those comments in which we are less interested. The danger of course, is that we may well be tuning out something that is important as well.

Second, our speed of thought is far higher than our talking speed. Most people talk at a rate of around 125 – 150 words per minute, but researchers have found that we think at the rate of around 500 words a minute. This leads us to jump ahead of what the speaker is saying, anticipating his next comments. If we are not doing this, we may be thinking of something else, giving our attention to what we are going to say next, or something that happened earlier in the day or which might happen tomorrow, or any one of a countless number of things.

The third factor which prevents us from listening as well as we might is simply a lack of interest in the subject matter. When this occurs, and we feel that the speaker is just droning on, we mentally switch off. It may take a really competent speaker to attract our attention when the subject matter is of little interest. Listening to the Radio 4 programme *From Our Own Correspondent*, or *International Assignment,* either of which may start with a report about some obscure conflict or situation on the other side of the world, I have frequently been poised to turn the off the radio. Then an arresting word or phrase might capture the imagination, and I find myself interested for the next 15 minutes or longer, the quality of the reporting (the writing, in fact) is that good. However, most of us have to listen to speakers who do not have the ability to capture our imaginations in that way, but we are still expected to listen. Making the effort is nearly always worthwhile, because there will almost certainly be something that you will learn or through which you might gain a fresh insight into the speaker's mind.

Another factor that impedes our listening ability occurs when the speaker displays some characteristic that we dislike. Then, instead of concentrating on *what is said*, we find ourselves thinking about *the person.* This is a common fault in those who interview – either for employment, counselling, or any other purpose. Few people interview objectively, concentrating on what is said, rather than what the candidate appears to be. Thus, when a candidate's appearance is other than what we expect, or when he has personal mannerisms that we dislike, we often allow these factors to distract us from paying attention to what he is saying. We judge the person, instead of that which he has to say.

So much for the potential distractions. Do others know when we are not listening? You bet. Our eyes glaze over and slip out of focus; we look past the speaker instead of at him; we start putting things away in a briefcase; we brush some imaginary dust from our clothing; we examine the floor, perhaps pretending to be thinking about what has been said. All these are signals of our lack of attention, and all of them will almost certainly be picked up by the speaker and interpreted as showing a lack of interest.

What effect might that have on a young player seeking advice? What might the effect be on a mature player, perhaps looking for reassurance or wanting your comments on a personal problem?

Industrial studies have shown that managers spend 45% – 65% of the time listening. Arguably, the percentage for the coach must be similar. So how do we become active listeners? There are a number of simple things we can do which will not only improve our listening skills, but may also help to cement better relationships with those with whom we come into contact.

First, focus on your own behaviour. Do you think about what you are going to say while the other person is still speaking? This is probably one of the basic faults for many of us, particularly so when we are aware that the subject demands an intelligent and considered response. Because of this, we plan the content of our response instead of listening to the speaker. Since the giving of advice is central to the role of the coach, he may feel that he is not doing his job unless he is also doing the talking. Another reason may lie in anxiety or a lack of self-confidence. The coach may be too eager to 'chip in', for example, to show the speaker that he understands the problem. If he withheld his comments a little longer, he might gain additional information that would enable him to make a more pertinent and considered reply.

Second, the listener's posture is a factor that can influence active listening. If we are sitting or standing in a slack or casual manner it can affect our attitude – and perhaps the attitude of the speaker. Active listening demands looking alert (but not tense), and *looking* interested as well as *being* interested. We have all had the experience of speaking to someone whose mind is obviously elsewhere, and when this occurs at a time when we need help or advice, we may have a feeling of being devalued. We also need to be sensitive to the other's voice and tone, and body language. A slack or casual posture on your part sends a strong signal. Studies by social psychologists have shown that such things as maintaining good posture and eye contact are regarded as important indicators of an active listener. Intriguingly, our posture affects attitudes and feelings, so if we *look* alert, we are more likely to *be* alert. Eye contact should be steady and even, but short of staring in an unblinking manner. (Note that people from some other cultures regard eye contact as impolite, and will therefore tend to avert their gaze.)

If you feel you are losing the sense of what the speaker is saying it is quite in order to interrupt for the sake of clarification. Phrases such as, *"so what you mean is...?"* or *"let me check my understanding so far..."* Such interruptions demonstrate that you are clearly interested in what the speaker has to say.

The psychological aspects of listening include paying attention to the speaker's non-verbal behaviour – facial expression, gestures, and posture – and to what is said and what is *not* said. When you are concentrating on these factors by giving your full attention, you will find also that your comprehension will increase. Try to listen to what is said in an objective but sympathetic manner. This is particularly important when a player has personal difficulties. If you can listen in a calm and objective manner, this in itself is likely to have a calming effect. When speakers become emotional over a problem, they may well interpret your calm and objective approach as 'coldness', so it is important to signify that you understand the problem and that you are not making hasty judgements.

Finally, you need to check your understanding of what is said. Make sure that you have grasped the central theme of the topic, even if the details may be less clear in your mind. Do not hesitate to ask clarifying questions. This is important in one-to-one discussions and even more important at meetings where many of us are reluctant to admit that we may not have grasped a particular point for fear of looking foolish. My own experience on such occasions has shown that almost invariably, others around the table have not grasped the point either. Having heard the speaker out, you need to take a 'helicopter view' of what has been said. What was the real purpose of the discussion? What has the speaker been explaining? What was his purpose? The answer could be a number of things:

- getting something 'off his chest'
- trying to clarify a situation
- trying to pursuade you to his way of thinking
- seeking advice about a technical problem connected with his performance
- seeking your agreement

These are just a few of the possibilities. You will be able to add more. It is necessary not just to analyse the words but to try to understand what the speaker's underlying intentions might be. You can do this only by constant attention and questioning in your own mind.

Verbal questioning is an important supplement, and can be used for a variety of purposes. Summarising questions are particularly useful:

*"So you think that...?"*

*"Am I right in believing that...?"*

Do not miss out on questions of clarification:

*"I'm not quite sure I got the point about..."*

*"I'm not clear on what you mean by..."*

Such questions will not only greatly increase your own comprehension but are likely to be appreciated by the speaker – they will give him a second chance to make his point!

The following questionnaire is designed to help you analyse your current listening skills as a coach. Before you develop your listening skills further, it is useful for you to have an awareness of where you are now.

Complete the questionnaire in 10 minutes. Note that you need to write down your initial 'gut feel' response. Do not write down what you think you ought to write – that will be a waste of your time.

# QUESTIONNAIRE

Complete the following. Take about 10 minutes and write what comes to you naturally. Be honest with yourself. Refer to the list occasionally to remind yourself of the key points.

1. I am happy to listen to a player when

. . . . . . . . . . . . . . . . . . . . . . . . . . . . . . . . . . .

. . . . . . . . . . . . . . . . . . . . . . . . . . . . . . . . . . .

2. I am usually friendly to a player who

. . . . . . . . . . . . . . . . . . . . . . . . . . . . . . . . . . .

. . . . . . . . . . . . . . . . . . . . . . . . . . . . . . . . . . .

3. I do not like players who

. . . . . . . . . . . . . . . . . . . . . . . . . . . . . . . . . . .

. . . . . . . . . . . . . . . . . . . . . . . . . . . . . . . . . . .

4. What irritates me most about a player is

. . . . . . . . . . . . . . . . . . . . . . . . . . . . . . . . . . .

. . . . . . . . . . . . . . . . . . . . . . . . . . . . . . . . . . .

5. I tend to switch off when a player talks about

. . . . . . . . . . . . . . . . . . . . . . . . . . . . . . . . . . .

. . . . . . . . . . . . . . . . . . . . . . . . . . . . . . . . . . .

6. The thing that prevents me from listening carefully to a player is when

. . . . . . . . . . . . . . . . . . . . . . . . . . . . . . . . . . .

. . . . . . . . . . . . . . . . . . . . . . . . . . . . . . . . . . .

7. I get annoyed when a player talks about

. . . . . . . . . . . . . . . . . . . . . . . . . . . . . . . . . . .

. . . . . . . . . . . . . . . . . . . . . . . . . . . . . . . . . . .

8. I enjoy listening to a  player talk about

. . . . . . . . . . . . . . . . . . . . . . . . . . . . . . . . . . .

. . . . . . . . . . . . . . . . . . . . . . . . . . . . . . . . . . .

9. I can concentrate better when a player is talking about

   . . . . . . . . . . . . . . . . . . . . . . . . . . . . . . . . .

   . . . . . . . . . . . . . . . . . . . . . . . . . . . . . . . . .

10. If I can't contribute to a conversation I feel

    . . . . . . . . . . . . . . . . . . . . . . . . . . . . . . . . .

    . . . . . . . . . . . . . . . . . . . . . . . . . . . . . . . . .

11. When a player talks about a subject with which I'm familiar, I

    . . . . . . . . . . . . . . . . . . . . . . . . . . . . . . . . .

    . . . . . . . . . . . . . . . . . . . . . . . . . . . . . . . . .

12. When a player talks about a cricket problem, I

    . . . . . . . . . . . . . . . . . . . . . . . . . . . . . . . . .

    . . . . . . . . . . . . . . . . . . . . . . . . . . . . . . . . .

13. When a player talks about domestic or personal problems, I

    . . . . . . . . . . . . . . . . . . . . . . . . . . . . . . . . .

    . . . . . . . . . . . . . . . . . . . . . . . . . . . . . . . . .

14. I try not to interrupt when a player is talking about

    . . . . . . . . . . . . . . . . . . . . . . . . . . . . . . . . .

    . . . . . . . . . . . . . . . . . . . . . . . . . . . . . . . . .

To listen to players better, perhaps I need to

   . . . . . . . . . . . . . . . . . . . . . . . . . . . . . . . . .

   . . . . . . . . . . . . . . . . . . . . . . . . . . . . . . . . .

   . . . . . . . . . . . . . . . . . . . . . . . . . . . . . . . . .

   . . . . . . . . . . . . . . . . . . . . . . . . . . . . . . . . .

# CHECK LIST FOR ACTIVE LISTENING

❖ Active listening is not the same as hearing.

❖ Active listening encourages the speaker to reveal more of his thoughts and increases the proportion that you positively hear.

❖ Most of us tend to be selective in our hearing by 'tuning out' those things which we think are less important.

❖ Our speed of thought is far higher than our talking speed, leading us to race ahead when someone is talking. Often, we might be thinking of what we are going to say next, rather than listening.

❖ Our lack of interest in the subject matter may make it difficult to listen actively, but if we try harder we might learn something.

❖ Concentrate on what is being said, not on the person saying it.

❖ Speakers can usually tell when the other person is not actively listening: consider that affect on a young cricketer or one seeking your support or advice.

❖ Be aware of your own behaviour whilst listening. Don't 'chip in' unnecessarily. *Look* as if you are interested in what is being said.

❖ Checking your understanding and seeking clarification will demonstrate your interest.

❖ Pay attention to what is *not* said.

❖ Summarise at the end.

# 12   Leadership

*A French general was once tactlessly asked, after a famous victory, if his second-in-command hadn't really won it. He thought for some time before answering. "Maybe so," he replied. "But one thing is certain: if the battle had been lost I would have lost it."*

Quoted by Mike Brearley in *The Art of Captaincy*

Leadership is really one aspect of communication and is primarily about what leaders *do* not what they *are*. A simplification certainly, but one with much truth in it. Leadership has to be communicated to the led through action of some kind.

*If a man runs into a room stark naked, painted blue, and proclaiming that the end of the world is nigh, he has escaped from the local asylum. If he is followed by fifty others doing the same thing, he is a leader.*

Jim Dercan

It is impossible to talk constructively about management – the management of anything from a cricket team to a multi-national organisation - for any length of time without raising the subject of leadership. Discussion inevitably leads to recitation of a long list of qualities desirable – if not essential – in a leader. The chances are that most of them will be right. More specifically, each quality may be right for a given situation with a given group at a particular point in time, but it has taken several decades for this truism to be recognised.

As a starting point, we might ask what we mean by leadership. Psychologists have advanced many definitions over the years, but for the cricket coach, perhaps the most helpful definition is *"the behaviour of an individual when directing the activities of a group toward a shared goal"*. In this chapter we will look at some of the leadership theories that have been proposed generally, and some specifically in relation to sport.

## Personality traits

Up until about the time of the Second World War, the 'great man' theory of leadership was prevalent. There was an assumption that effective leaders were born with a set of personality traits, which were conducive to leadership – traits such as intelligence, assertiveness and independence. Personality traits are regarded as characteristics with which one is born, and as such are relatively stable over time. After the war there was a move towards the *'situation specific'* theory, perhaps because the war had thrown up many examples of high leadership by ordinary mortals, leading to the belief that there were aspects of leadership behaviour which could be learned.

Compare personality traits with *leadership behaviours* – which are about what leaders might do in specific situations. Leadership behaviours are specific to a given situation and may have little relevance to other situations. Clearly this has many implications. First, it gives hope to those of us who were not born with the prescribed quantities of intelligence, assertiveness, and independence referred to earlier. Second, it implies that we can acquire those skills (behaviours) necessary to leadership.

The first personality test – the Woodworth Personality Data Sheet - was introduced in 1917 and was successfully used to identify emotionally unstable soldiers. World War II saw a very considerable expansion in the use of psychological tests, and these were coupled with two or three days of practical exercises, often designed to elicit leadership qualities, and which were later to develop into what we now refer to as assessment or development centres. During the last fifty years or so, psychologists have come round to the view that there is little evidence to support the existence of a *universal* leadership trait theory either in industry at large or in sport.

It is important to distinguish between *leadership traits* and *leadership behaviours.* As mentioned above, traits are fairly stable aspects of personality, remaining very much the same during our lifetime. Assertiveness, independence, and intelligence are three such traits. Conscientiousness and confidence are two more. Leadership behaviours are concerned with what leaders do - how they behave when in a position of leadership. It was probably this factor that led the late John Garnett of The Industrial Society to state that leadership is about what leaders *do*, not what they *are*.

## Leadership and sport

One psychologist[1] has proposed two distinct approaches to the theory of leadership in sport.

First, there is the *influence system*. This approach suggests that the coach and the sportsman influence each other in the way in which they accomplish goals. Hence, coaches do not work in isolation: they are influenced by the situation in which they find themselves as well as by the players themselves.

Second, there is the *power system* in which the coach tends to isolate himself from the players. He communicates only at a minimum level and such communication as there is will flow from him to the players, rather than as a two-way system of expressing feelings, doubts, and concerns. This style of management is now fairly antiquated but was certainly alive in soccer until a few years ago, when social conditions - players' wages, and a greater deference to authority - were very different than they are today.

A further difference in leadership theories lies in the distinction to be drawn between an appointed leader, and an emergent leader. In sport, the leader (coach) is usually appointed but may have difficulty in being accepted if his values, style, technical knowledge, etc., do not match the expectations of the players. In clubs where there is a less structured approach - amateur sports clubs, for example - a leader might emerge. Two psychologists conducted an experiment to determine whether an appointed leader or an emergent leader was most effective - each was in charge of a group of students. The task was for the students to find their way blind-folded through a maze. The belief was that the group with the appointed leader would do best, because his leadership was established and there were proper lines of communication. In the event the group with the emergent leader did best, because the leader had knowledge and skills which quickly became evident as the task progressed. The appointed leader had no such skills but since he *was recognised* as being the leader, no other leader emerged. The significance of this is clear: a leader is most effective when there is a situation specifically requiring his or her skills. Thus a leader with so-called leadership skills might be successful in some tasks and some of the time, but is unlikely to be successful in all leadership tasks all the time. The rise of the emergent leader might be summed up in the phrase *"Cometh the hour, cometh the man."*

Personality traits that are evident in all successful leaders are *universal* traits, and those that are specific to one situation are known as *situation specific* traits. Therefore it follows that a coach or captain who displays high leadership skills at cricket might not show the necessary leadership skills in an industrial or commercial organisation. They may both be management jobs but the ingredients for success might be very different. However, there is an optimistic side to this: if successful leadership behaviours can be identified they can also be learned. So you don't have to be born great - you might just have greatness thrust upon you by the situation in which you find yourself! Cricket coaches can acquire behaviours that are likely to lead to success by studying the practices of those coaches already recognised as highly successful.

## Two important factors

In the late 1940s two American Universities, Ohio State University and the University of Michigan, studied leadership and independently, arrived at very similar conclusions. As a result, leadership research took a new direction. Instead of focusing on *universal traits*, it focused on *universal behaviours*, leading to the conclusion that leaders *can be made, not born.* They found that the two most important factors in successful leadership were *consideration and initiating structure.*

Consideration refers to a leader's behaviour that is indicative of friendship, trust, respect, and warmth. It will be democratic, with a focus on people.

Initiating structure refers to behaviour that is focused on getting the job done – e.g. ensuring that lines of communication are clear, and that the team is well-organised. It signifies a more directive - perhaps even autocratic and authoritarian - style in which subordinates are left in no doubt about the organisation, channels of communication, and methods of procedure. There will be a strong focus on the task.

The message for the leader is clear: coaches should pay attention to factors such as communication and organisation but also display those behaviours associated with warmth, friendliness, and respect and trust.

Many psychologists and management thinkers have picked up these two factors -consideration and initiating structure - since the 1950s. Douglas McGregor advanced his Theory X and Theory Y styles of management in 1960[2], the Theory X being task-centred and Theory Y being people-centred. (See Chapter Three.) A similar theory was put forward later by Blake and Mouton[3]. This theory identifies a *concern for people* and a *concern for task* and although managers may prefer one of these styles to the other, the key point is that they are not mutually exclusive. It is possible to be high on both, as they are independent variables. For example a coach who involved his players in determining a strategy or course of action would be showing a concern for the task (how do you think we should do it?) and a concern for his players (let's work together on this.)

## Coaching behaviour

Some sport psychologists have studied the behaviour of coaches, and early studies indicated that coaching behaviour is characterised by dominance, aggression and authoritarianism. This was later confounded in the mid-1970s in a study of hockey coaches, which found that successful coaches placed an emphasis on communication. In the 1980s, a questionnaire known as the Leadership Scale for Sports was developed, and subsequently used amongst competitive rowers. Here it became apparent that those who were younger and less skilled had a clear preference for a coach who paid attention to them as individuals (the consideration factor referred to above.) Sportsmen who were highly skilled and mature also preferred the consideration style of coaching in preference to the initiating structure approach. After all, they have mastered their sport and are therefore likely to respond to a coaching style that recognises this. It seems therefore, that the coach needs to adopt a style which reflects consideration for younger, less mature players, and the more highly skilled and experienced, leaving those in the middle ground to respond best to the initiating structure approach.

The results of other research conducted since have clearly shown that successful coaching behaviours can be identified and learned. This needs to be capitalised upon within cricket through the systematic study of successful cricket coaches as leaders with the results being fed into the national coaching scheme.

Some researchers have been dissatisfied with the consideration-initating structure approach, because it did not identify either personality traits or behaviours that consistently pinpointed differences between effective and non-effective leaders. A set of traits or behaviours that were successful in one set of circumstances did not necessarily lead to success in another.

## Fiedler's Contingency Theory

Fiedler's[4] contingency theory states that effective leadership is contingent upon the leader's personality traits and the degree to which the situation allows the leader to exert his influence. The leader (coach) may either be biased towards strengthening relationships between him and the group, or he may be task-centred, meaning that the completion of the task would be his priority and therefore receive the most attention. The situational element relates to the degree to which the leader can exercise control and influence over the group, the type of task, and the degree of authority the leader can exercise to reward or punish. The theory states that this last factor is the *least* important, and the relationship between the leader and the group is the *most* important. All these elements will determine the type of leadership behaviour that is most likely to attain the group's objectives.

### Characteristics of leaders

|  |  | *Traits* | *Behaviours* |
|---|---|---|---|
| 1 | *More general* | Trait or 'great man' theory | American University studies |
| 2 | *More specific* | Fiedler's Contingency theory | Situation-specific theories |

**Figure 7**
Four types of leadership theories

There have been a number of other studies into leadership in the last twenty-five years or so. One of them, the path-goal theory,[5] is worthy of consideration in the context of sport. This theory underlines the importance of the needs and objectives of the player, and the coach becomes a facilitator. Whether or not the coach is regarded as successful, depends on whether the player - or the team - reaches its goals. According to this theory, the coach would give encouragement

- an intrinsic reward – to those who achieve their objectives. Difficulties and problems would be highlighted and likely to be resolved through a joint approach.

Another approach to the question of leadership in sport was advanced by the *life-cycle theory*[6]. As with the path-goal theory, the emphasis is on the player and the team, rather than the leader, and hinges on the maturity of the player. Maturity in this sense refers not to age, but to the player's willingness to set personal goals, to pursue them conscientiously, and generally to assume responsibility for his own development. As mentioned earlier, *Task structure* behaviour decreases in proportion to the increase in maturity. In other words, the more mature the player, the less need there is for the disciplined approach mentioned earlier. The need for *consideration* – emphasising relationships, friendliness etc., is at its highest when players are new and when they are mature. The middle ground is more likely to demand a task structure approach. It would seem therefore, that for the best results, the coach's behaviour should be related to the maturity level of the player or players.

## Compatibility

The degree of compatibility between a coach and a player is an important factor, and it is perfectly possible to measure this with an assessment questionnaire known as FIRO B, developed by Will Schutz in the late 1950s. This measures three dimensions of interpersonal relations – Inclusion, Control, and Affection. Each of these can be divided into what we express to others, and that which we want in return. Inclusion refers to the extent to which one wishes to be involved with others; Control deals with the extent to which one desires control and influence over other people; Affection refers to the degree of warmth that we express to others and want in return.

This assessment has been used to determine not just whether a coach and a player are compatible, but to spotlight the specific areas in which they appear to be incompatible. Thus, on Inclusion, one of the parties might show a preference for relatively little contact with others – initiating this behaviour and requiring little involvement in return. He would therefore seem to be incompatible with a player whose needs on this dimension appeared to be very high.

There are further distinctions to be made: between elected leaders and appointed leaders, for example. The sports coach is certainly in a leadership position by appointment, and those who appoint him may not be those most immediately affected by his leadership style. Every functioning group needs a leader, and the members will expect the group to be properly led. The two aspects of this role are the activities comprising the role, and the style in which they are carried out. Take a few minutes to think of the activities of the following:

- a trade union leader
- the manager of a professional football team
- the leader of a youth club
- the chief executive of a national charity
- the managing director of a manufacturing company
- the commanding officer of an army unit

Possible activities might for each in turn, might be:

- ensuring that members understand the current industrial relations issues
- projecting a positive approach to the media on behalf of the club
- constantly searching for new ways to maintain the interest of members
- making the public aware of the need for voluntary donations
- deploying all company resources to maximum effect
- instilling a sense of regimental pride and comradeship

## Activities of leader

It is important to distinguish between the work of the group and the activities of the leader. If the leader becomes too involved in the work of the group, i.e. the tasks, it will certainly generate friction and maybe resentment on the part of group members. The activities of the leader should be directed at those things which the group members are less able to do effectively. The way in which the leader carries out these activities will demonstrate his *style* of leadership. Some management theorists advocate that a distinction be made between the leader whose job it is to create a 'vision', and the management who determine the way in which that vision will become a reality.

If the cricket coach concentrates too much on the task, he will almost certainly receive objections from the captain; if he concentrates too much on the style he is in danger of alienating supporters and spectators who will be pressing for results. The coach needs to concentrate on both aspects equally, seeking to weld the team into a cohesive whole, whilst focusing on competitive success.

Mike Hendrick, veteran of 30 Tests for England and now National Coach for the Scottish Cricket Union, summed it up when he said, *"The coach must be versatile. You have to be able to do a wide variety of things."*


## Leadership style

Leadership style is all-important, and is best thought of as a continuum, with an authoritarian style at one end, and a consensus, or participative style at the other. The figure 8 illustrates a range of styles, each of which might be relevant and necessary in a given situation.

Defining what leadership might be is certainly more difficult than defining what it is not. It is not, for example, about setting a style that is completely at odds with the social norms of the day, and football management in the 60s and 70s provide examples which contrast starkly with present practices.

Manchester United, currently the most successful and the wealthiest football club in the world, was built on the foundations laid by Sir Matt Busby, and in a television programme about Busby, the current manager, Sir Alex Ferguson, acknowledged this. Busby, like all legendary managers, had more than a streak of ruthlessness behind the easy charm. He was able to indulge some of his excesses simply because of the values of his day. Players had no agents, contracts were binding, and their egos were not inflated by excessive wages. Indeed, Busby filled in the figures in his players' contracts. No negotiation here. When Denis Law tried to set out his terms, he was immediately placed on the transfer list. Managers no longer have that power, and even Sir Alex Ferguson may now have to cosset players whom he wants to keep. Roy Keane's wage rise to £52,000 per week is ample evidence of this.

Alf Ramsey, Bill Shankly, Bob Paisley and Jock Stein, all great football managers, emulated the Busby managerial style in an age in which deference to authority was still evident. For Shankly, the greatest crime was to be injured which he took to be a sign of weakness.

**Figure 8**
Leadership
style

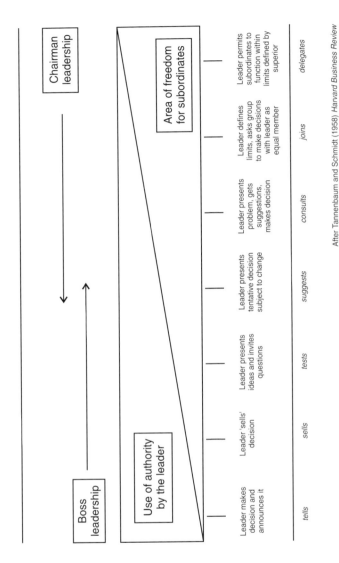

After Tannenbaum and Schmidt (1958) *Harvard Business Review*

Paisley succeeded him, and under his management Liverpool won 13 trophies in 9 years. But the 'hard man' style of management continued and when Keegan signed for Hamburg, Paisley tried to ensure that he never again played for England.

Jock Stein was in a similar mould. Apparently he commanded respect at Celtic but, according to a former player, *"he had this ability to shrink you with a torrent of abuse and the next minute make you feel ten-feet tall."* When a player was dropped from a game, he was never given a reason, and was not expected to ask for one.

Brian Clough, at the height of his fame at Nottingham Forest, was asked how he dealt with disagreements. He said, *"We sit down and talk about it for maybe 20 minutes. Then we do it my way."* "My way, or the highway," sums it up.

What can we learn from these hard styles of leadership? They produced results certainly, but they must be seen as suitable for a particular era when values – for better or worse – were different from those of today

Listen to Steve Oldham, of Yorkshire CCC:

*"Since going to Bradford, I've felt that much of what we have been doing was wrong. I was brought up in an environment where you gave orders. 'This is how you do it.' I've learned that there are other ways, like giving boys ownership and letting them tell me when they need help. My advice to schoolmasters who coach cricket is to encourage boys to take ownership of the game. I've done this and it's a lot less stressful for me. I think boys are tougher on themselves than I might be. For example we have a slow left-armer whose run-up was at a sharp right angle to the crease so his balance was poor. I suggested he straightened his run-up to give himself a better approach. I asked him how much more comfortable his run-up now felt. He started marking himself out of ten for feeling comfortable. When he got to ten, he gave himself marks for his leading arm and his head. He started giving himself six and then within half an hour it was ten. That way will work with younger people."*

Another example of changing attitudes is exemplified by England captain Nasser Hussain giving an interview to a magazine and thus providing an insight into his psychological approach to handling the so-called 'problem boys' of the squad.

*"For a large percentage of the time, everyone in the England team has to do the same thing – what they wear, the time they turn up, the looseners we do before a match. But I think you have to start on an individual basis, then go out to the team ethic. Tufnell is a classic*

*example of that. He is, I think, a little bit of a genius. But he's doing his own art. So you let him go off and prepare how he wants and then drag him in. When he turns up for a Test Match, you can't get him into a Team England mode straight away by saying 'You're here, you've got to do this at nine o'clock, this at half-nine, you can't do anything differently and, if you don't abide by these rules, goodbye.' I suspect his immediate reaction would be 'Well sod you, I do things my own way,' and he'd become a bit of a rebel. Whereas if you gave him a bit of leeway, he'll be there when you asked him to be. I don't believe in laying down lots of rules as if they're all schoolboys. It's not up to me to come in and start saying 'You're going to do this and you're going to do that.' At the moment we've got people like Tufnell and Andrew Caddick. who do things differently. People forget that they may be good cricketers because they do things differently."*

Today we need to practice *contingency theory*. This simply means that you do what needs to be done in the *light of the circumstances at the time* - not as part of some rigidly applied dogma.

# CHECK LIST FOR LEADERSHIP

❖ Until about the time of the Second World War the "great man" theory of leadership prevailed. This assumed that leaders were born and not made. In other words, they were born with certain personality characteristics that appeared relevant when placed in a position of leadership.

❖ In the early 1950s this theory lost favour and researchers advanced the idea that leadership qualities were "situation specific". The way a leader *behaved* in a given situation was thought to be more important than his inborn personality characteristics.

❖ Behaviour is visible, and can be studied, analysed, copied, and taught. Personality characteristics are not visible.

❖ The *influence theory* proposes that the coach and the player be influenced by each other as well as the situation in which they find themselves.

❖ The *power system* proposes that the coach is somewhat detached from the players and that communication is largely one way. This style of management may work in specific situations but it is unlikely to be successful in an age when respect for authority figures does not come naturally to many people.

❖ A leader is likely to be most effective when there is a situation that specifically demands his skills.

❖ Leadership studies at two American universities in the 1950s identified two important ingredients of successful coaches (therefore, leaders). These were *consideration* and *initiating structure*. Consideration is a concern for people – showing trust, warmth, respect. Initiating structure refers to the organisation, the channels of communication, and other factors required to achieve the task.

- ❖ Players who are beginners, and also those who are highly skilled and experienced, are more likely to respond favourably to a coaching style that emphasises consideration. – a concern for people. Those in an intermediate position might respond better to the "initiating structure" approach.

- ❖ Fiedler's contingency theory states that effective leadership is dependent on the leader's personality traits and the degree to which the situation allows him to exercise them.

- ❖ The *path-goal theory* refers to the objectives and needs of the player with the coach as a facilitator. His success depends on whether the player achieves his objectives.

- ❖ The *life-cycle theory* places the emphasis on the player and the team rather than the coach. This approach requires a degree of maturity – self-discipline, conscientiousness in goal setting, etc., for it to succeed.

- ❖ Leadership styles may vary from age to age. It not only has to be relevant for the situation, but it needs to be acceptable to the 'followers'.

# 13  Teamwork

*Adieu, fond game, whose many friendships wove*
*Around thy lover's heart a net of love,*
*Where all have been joy, harmony, and peace,*
*Until my grave, love for thee shall not cease.*

*Adieu, Fond Game*
An Old Cricketer

Teamwork … the buzzword of the 90s – and no doubt of the new century. On first thoughts it might be surprising that much of what we know about the functioning of teams comes not from sport but from business. Business has borrowed the word from sport and it is in the business context that most of the studies on teamwork in this country have been conducted. It is however, something of a paradox. Teamwork surely, should be found in its purest form in those sports that are built around the team concept – football, rugby and basketball, certainly. Cricket to some extent, although it relies on individual performances within a team context. There appear to be two reasons for this paradox. First, sport at the highest level does not easily lend its teamwork element to psychological study. Most coaches and club officials would be loath to allow a researcher to conduct a study with the scientific control and rigour that would be necessary to produce meaningful results. Second, business has developed an interest in teamwork largely, though not exclusively, due to the introduction of Japanese management practices into the UK.

On the face of it, the reader may think that there is not much to research. After all, is it not just a case of some like-minded people working together towards some agreed objective? Well, behind such a simple statement lies an abundance of assumptions on which some sport psychologists have worked for decades, and a few of them will be introduced in this chapter. But first, before we look at these, let us look more closely at the work of Dr. R. Meredith Belbin[1].

## Belbin's Theory

Within the industrial and commercial field, his work stands out, and is well worthy of the attention of coaches as well as sport psychologists.

In the 1970s Belbin was closely concerned with the senior executive management course run at the Administrative Staff College, Henley, more succinctly known simply as Henley, the oldest management college in Europe. Here, for some aspects of the course, senior managers would need to break into eight syndicates with six managers in each, to participate in a management simulation game. Each syndicate represented a company, and the results of the business simulation exercise which they were asked to conduct, were measurable. Managers attending the course were bankers, engineers, scientists, accountants, civil servants and managers with production or commercial experience – all practising managers and with the sort of potential for the highest management positions which justified their being released for eight or ten weeks. The 'output' from the simulation game was a profit or loss and therefore the companies could be compared with one another.

What intrigued Belbin, and led to his continued research into teamwork over the ensuing years, was the varying degree of success with which this management game was played. They were all intelligent people – so why were some successful, and others not? Was it because the brightest people had somehow been assembled into the same group? Belbin and his colleagues began to study the makeup of the team members. To do this he used a range of psychometric tests together with skilled observers, and the comments and behaviour of the team members were monitored. Belbin says, *"Some unsuccessful companies had avoided examining the underlying reasons for their poor results by seizing on gratifying excuses. The favourites were* 'If the game had gone on longer, we would have won,' *and* 'We would have done all right if it hadn't been for some doubtful umpiring on a critical point.' (So attribution theory is not confined to sport!)

The outcome of Belbin's research programme was that he identified nine team roles necessary for successful team performance. Each team role type has its strengths and its allowable weaknesses. They are: PLANT (creative, imaginative, comes up ideas); RESOURCE INVESTIGATOR (extravert, enthusiastic, explores opportunities, develops contacts); CO-ORDINATOR (mature, confident, clarifies goals, delegates well); SHAPER (challenging, dynamic, thrives on pressure, overcomes obstacles); MONITOR EVALUATOR (sober, strategic, discerning, sees all the options, judges accurately); TEAMWORKER (co-operative, mild, perceptive, diplomatic, listens, averts friction); IMPLEMENTER (disciplined, reliable efficient, turns ideas into practical action); COMPLETER (painstaking, conscientious, anxious, searches out errors); SPECIALIST (single-minded, self-starting, dedicated, provides expertise in rare supply). (The Belbin Team Role Profile Sheet appears at Appendix 2).

This does not imply that a successful team must contain nine people, one for each team role type. One person might be competent say, both as a Teamworker and as an Implementer, but could also take on the role of Completer if necessary. The Belbin Team Role Self-Perception Inventory (an assessment devised in the 1980s, following the identification of these team types), also highlights the team role type that an individual should avoid – the 'least preferred' role. It is as important to be aware of this, as it is to be aware of one's natural role.

The whole point of Belbin's theory of course, is that a successful team should be built around a *diversity* of personality types, each contributing its own strengths. However, there are other approaches to team building and other assessments that can be used for the purpose, notably the Myers Briggs Type Indicator (MBTI)™, which is appropriate where the requirement is that of *compatibility* between team members. This would be relevant for a small team of two or three, where a reasonable degree of like-mindedness is likely to assist in the smooth completion of a project.

I have asked many professional coaches for their views on teamwork, and not surprisingly, received a wide range of answers. Hugh Morris, Technical Director of the ECB thinks the Belbin Team Role Types have some applicability to cricket. He recalled his time as captain of Glamorgan when they won the Britannic Assurance County Championship in 1997, when Duncan Fletcher was coach, prior to his England appointment. How did they approach teamwork, I asked?

> *"There was plenty of discussion about tactics and strategy. Everyone was allowed to have his say and everyone knew what he was supposed to do. The teamwork developed into team spirit. Duncan Fletcher shaped the path of the season, and both junior and senior players were involved. Once the plan was laid, each person knew what he had to do, and that led to good team spirit."*

## Group cohesion

That might describe teamwork, but what is a team? First of course, it is more than a collection of individuals. As soon as people come together in a team it no longer relates to the outside world as its individuals might. Group behaviour is always different from individual behaviour. The team becomes a separate and distinct entity. When a team is successful its members will enjoy working together as they will be attracted to each other – perhaps because of their like-mindedness. It is a very appealing hypothesis therefore, to believe that if people enjoy playing sport together, and they like each other, they will form a successful team. Put another way, is a successful team a harmonious team? Unfortunately – but intriguingly – this is not always the case. The history of sport abounds with examples of successful teams with disharmony in the ranks. Football has been rife with it, and the comment that "the dressing room was split down the middle," will be familiar to close followers of cricket.

Sport psychologists talk of *team cohesion* and by this, they mean the manner in which members of a team interact with each other. In other words, it is the 'glue' which holds the group together. However, this takes no account of the changing nature of a team and the importance of its objectives. Albert Carron[2] has advanced a better definition: *"a dynamic process which is reflected in the tendency for a group to stick together and remain united in pursuit of goals and objectives."*

There are two aspects of group cohesion: those factors that contribute to cohesion in the first place (known as the determinants), and the success or failure of that cohesion (known as the consequences.)

*Social cohesion* refers to the extent that members of a team are able to get along with each other, sometimes referred to as social attraction. *Task cohesion* refers to the extent to which team members are prepared to work together to achieve a specific task – in cricket, to score runs and take wickets.

These two team 'ingredients' can operate independently of each other. We have referred elsewhere to teams that have been successful in spite of rifts as in Yorkshire and Surrey in the 1950s. Team chemistry seems to defy definition. On a much smaller scale, Torvill and Dean, former world and Olympic ice dance champions, were reportedly not well suited off the ice rink, but when performing together they were incomparable.

So: team cohesion has at least two elements to it (social and task cohesion.) The cricket coach needs to be aware that a team can be low on say, social cohesion and high on task cohesion. Task cohesion is likely to have a positive impact on performance, whilst social cohesion is thought to have a lesser affect.

Over the years, many studies have resulted in conclusions that seem to be contradictory, some concluding that co-operation within the team was the best predictor of success, and some concluding that competition was better.

In small groups, co-operation is more helpful in achieving success. The larger the group, the more difficult it is to co-operate fully. Of course, some sports demand more co-operation than do others: teams in archery or skiing require little co-operation and football and rugby require high co-operation. So much is obvious.

So co-operation is important to varying degrees dependent on the sport. Healthy competition however, should not be overlooked. Nor should the levels of self-esteem amongst the players. High self-esteem has been shown to be an important element of successful teams.

The results of studies over recent years confirm that both co-operation and competition are necessary, and that co-operation is closely allied to task cohesion. There are other factors that go to make up team cohesion and high performance. The stability of the team is one, and researchers have shown that teams whose members have stayed together for a reasonable length of time are more successful. Eighteen German football teams were studied during one season and the results showed that those who changed their players the least were more successful. Teams need time to develop cohesion for peak performance. There is of course, an optimum period, beyond which performance will suffer due to players ageing and losing form. Researchers tracked six major league baseball teams from 1901 to 1965 charting the composition of the teams and their success. The study showed that the optimum life was around five years, and that teams whose 'life span' was longer or shorter than this were less successful.

In summary, we can say that there is a distinct relationship between performance and team cohesion, particularly in sports that demand a degree of co-operation – and cricket is certainly one of those. But does team performance fuel team cohesion or does team cohesion fuel performance? (Note that here we are referring to performance, not success. A team may perform well, but lose to a superior team, or lose because of a bad umpiring decision, for example.) In the

1970s a series of studies measured team cohesion in several baseball teams at the start of a season, and at the end. The results showed that whilst team cohesion was high at the beginning, and thus helped team performance, it was even higher at the end of the season, indicating that high performance led to even higher team cohesion.

From this we can conclude that although team cohesion is highly desirable, it is possibly overrated as a contributor to success, high performance being more powerful.

In order to assist team cohesion, the coach might like to consider the following: -

- *Encourage the team to develop a feeling of ownership.* John Emburey recalls how under Mike Brearley's captaincy, players were encouraged to contribute ideas. On one occasion Brearley approached Norman Cowans and asked him what he thought the tactics should be at that particular point in the game. Cowans said that he didn't know. A few hours later Brearley asked him again by which time Cowans had some ideas, and was now therefore, more involved in the game. Brearley would frequently ask players for their views; often their views would coincide with his, but he did not say so. He let the player take the credit for the suggestion.
- *Get to know the players.* Not just the obvious facts, but something personal to each one.
- *Ensure that each player is aware of the responsibilities of the others.* One way to do this is to allow them to swap positions in practice. Let them know, for example, what it might feel like to keep wicket.
- *Do not expect the team to always be completely harmonious.* It is unrealistic. They are human beings, but the coach should certainly do his best to prevent cliques from developing, thereby leaving some in the 'out' group.
- *Give praise where it is due, even if the team lost.* Find something that was good about the performance.

## The complexity of teamwork

So much for the team, but what about the individual players? What is it that enables us to fit into a team? What are the essential characteristics? Even more intriguingly, why is it that we may fit into one team and not in another? After all, we are the same people. Aren't we? Well, perhaps not… Many factors influence the type of team role with which we feel most comfortable. Our main personality traits are probably the most influential, and this would include such factors as whether we are inclined to be more extravert or more introvert, and whether we are more anxious or less anxious in our everyday lives. Few of us behave completely naturally in every situation. We adjust according to the needs of the moment. For example, we probably behave differently at an interview than we would normally (partly because it is an artificial situation.) We are in effect acting out a role, whether we realise it or not. The behaviour we exhibit has been learned. It is the same in teamwork. If we feel, for example, that it is important that our actions and decisions are logical – in other words this might be one of our core values - this would affect our team role behaviour. If we have an innovative turn of mind, but find ourselves in an organisation where new ideas seem unwelcome, it is likely that in the long term we may just give up coming forward with new ideas, or we may simply leave. If we stay, we will be conforming to the perceived culture of the organisation (new ideas not welcome here). Thus, our natural team role, that of being the person to generate new ideas, will have been modified. I asked Steve, a bright manager from a world famous organisation how he was getting on, having almost completed his MBA. His face darkened.

*"We're like charcoal burners in the forest,"* he said. *"Every time I come up with a spark of a new idea, someone douses it with cold water. I'm seriously thinking of leaving."*

As Belbin[3] notes, our team role behaviour is enormously complex:

> *"Individuals eventually arrive at a stable pattern of association with their fellows based on a personal propensity, modified by the thought process, modified still further by personal values, governed by perceived constraints, influenced by experience, and added to by sophisticated learning."*

Still think teamwork is simple?

Before leaving Belbin's concept of team roles, it is worth looking at what he advocates (1993) when relationships within a team are strained.

157

> What happens when people are locked together by force
> of circumstance in a working association into which
> [neither] with any advanced knowledge would have entered
> freely? Can anything be done to stabilise their relationship?
> The situation may be likened to having to bat on a sticky
> wicket where a different style of strokeplay is required.
> To continue the analogy from cricket, a century is no longer
> the target. It is more a question of how to survive to score
> a few more runs. In such circumstances the achievement
> of a modest score can be the mark of a great batsman. So
> also, the ability to handle difficult individuals to some limited
> advantage is what distinguishes those who have special
> skills in people management.

Belbin goes on to say that it is difficult to establish a relationship with anybody without finding something that can be liked or admired. It is however, other people's shortcomings that we see first. *"Weaknesses in one particular area then tend to be generalised and our prejudices can prevent any later recognition of personal assets."* He believes that the most constructive approach is to look at the problem from another angle – *reframing* as psychologists call it. Start with something positive. Looking at the 'allowable weaknesses' may offer a clue as to a possible strength that you have yet to discover (see Appendix 2). As an example, the allowable weakness of the Plant is that he is unlikely to be good at communicating with those who do not share his interests. This is because the Plant is usually preoccupied with thoughts and innovative ideas in his own area of special interest. In other words he may talk animatedly on a topic with someone on his own wavelength, but he is less interested in small talk. A key point therefore, might be to find out what his special area of interest might be. What topic really enthuses him? Once that has been established, at least there is something to build upon, and the relationship may become more productive than it may otherwise would.

Many organisations interested in raising productivity through building productive teams, have sent managers on team building courses which frequently have a strong 'outdoors' element to them, many modelled on the Outward Bound concept developed in the immediate post-war years. These have their place, particularly in helping the development of younger people, but what is certain is that unless the values of the organisation truly espouse the concept of teamworking, the money will be wasted. To spend a week working as part of a team and then to return to a work environment in which teamworking may at best simply be an afterthought is all too common. To mean anything at all, the concept needs to be evident at every level in the organisation – including cricket clubs! It needs to be woven into the fabric of the management structure, and even now, at the start of a new century, and in spite of all the corporate talk about teamwork, there are relatively few organisations that can truly say that they endorse this concept throughout. They seem to value competitiveness far more.

The question is bound to arise, as to whether *everyone* can fit into a team, regardless of any other considerations. What about the maverick, the loner?

Before we despair, it is worth noting that the more obvious type of person who seems unlikely to fit into a team, might be the Plant (ideas generator) or the Specialist (has rare skills or knowledge). Although they are not obvious team types, they certainly have a role to play. Henry was an engineer and a specialist in diesel engines. He was an acknowledged expert, and his office gave ample evidence of his scholarship: it was packed from floor to ceiling on one side with books and magazines about diesel engines. He sat on just about every relevant committee in Europe, and was highly respected. He was not an easy person to get along with however. He was a Specialist and a Completer *par excellence.* (see Appendix 3.) The company started to look for his replacement 6 – 12 months before his retirement. His boss and other managers were adamant that they did not want 'another Henry', much as they respected him. He was too difficult; too attentive to minor issues. They produced a comprehensive list of characteristics thought to be essential in Henry's replacement and they were keyed into the computer. Albert had already been assessed, and yes, you guessed it… the computer said that Henry was the ideal candidate. Moral? Oddball characters with specialist skills may be essential to a team even if they are difficult. It is a trade off – their skills and knowledge on the one hand, and their difficult personalities on the other.


## Contention

But is teamwork just a question of being team-oriented or being competitive? Of each one singing from the same hymn book or of competitive destructiveness? Perhaps the missing factor is that of *contention*. To use another illustration from industry, Pascale believes that the best companies are those which encourage a degree of contention. In the *Art of Japanese Management*[1], he quotes Honda as one of the world's best-managed companies, and one in which the spirit of enquiry, or contention, is much in evidence, but in a controlled manner.

So perhaps in sport, we need those who will put forward a different point of view, who are prepared to argue their case. At least it demonstrates involvement.

Nasser Hussain gave an interview in which he said:

> *"If you're surrounded by yes-men nodding all the time, then nothing gets resolved. Of course at the end of the day it's important that I get my own way. The bare facts are that if the team doesn't win and is not successful, the buck stops with me. But I think in the past we've concentrated too much on the team ethic and not cared enough about individuals and how they perform and react."*

How common is it to have a cricket side that is completely harmonious? One coach I spoke to thought that it was almost impossible to have complete harmony. How can you achieve it with twelve or thirteen players, he asked?

He supplied the answer himself. He had one player who was particularly difficult, but the team worked out how to cope with him. In part, this was because he was playing well, and the rest of the team knew that although he was 'difficult', 99% of his efforts were directed towards the interests of the team, so they tolerated him.

Bob Appleyard, former England and Yorkshire seamer and off-spinner, recalls some of his former team-mates – Johnny Wardle, Fred Trueman and himself, all competing for wickets. *"They had strong ideas, and there were disagreements, but when on the field there was something unique – we worked for each other although we were competing for wickets. Johnny Wardle would be at one end and me the other. Teamwork is based on skills. You need the skills first and foremost and then comes the teamwork. Knowledge and skill breeds success and that leads to team spirit."*

Jack Birkenshaw's Leicestershire team won the championship in 1996. What were the ingredients of that success? Jack said, *"First, we had a caring type of captain and he was generous towards his players. Jimmy Whittaker had total belief in them. Everybody wanted to play. Whatever type of day it was – cold, wet – they all wanted to play cricket. They all enjoyed coming through the gate at Grace Road. They all looked forward to being away and going out for a meal together in the evening. They looked forward to a game of soccer together. They were a team on and off the field."*

Of course there can be a number of teamwork problems that lie outside the immediate influence of the coach. I put to one coach, what I thought might be a hypothetical question. I asked what might be the effect on a young cricketer who had received 'star status' at school and junior levels, and made the county side, only to find that he is relatively insignificant? *"Funny you should say that,"* he replied, and went on to give me an example of the son of a famous cricketer who had grown up hearing much about his father's contemporaries – many of them being outstanding cricketers of the day. He spoke about many of these famous names – *ad nauseum*. Of course, hardly any of the players knew these characters and the team clearly showed their displeasure.

A problem of a different type can occur when a player is drafted into a team at very short notice. Will his inclusion affect the cohesiveness of the team?

Mark Crossley missed 22 league games for Nottingham Forest before being told at 1.15 p.m. on the day of a crucial relegation match that he would be in goal. He brought off some spectacular saves including a late penalty, earning his team a draw and a desperately needed point. How did he adjust to a top class performance so quickly after being on the bench for so long?

As mentioned elsewhere, Nottinghamshire's Paul Johnson believes that team cohesiveness came from a belief in the ability of every other player in the team. To contradict this though, Paul felt that team spirit often comes from adversity. Certainly what might make good team spirit more likely is that of having a common goal, a common enemy, and common hardships. This is also the view of Kauss[5].

However, for all that we advocate team spirit, and enthuse about its desirability, there is plenty of scope for more research in this field. As we have already seen, social psychologists have not yet been able to show conclusively that teams with strong team cohesion *necessarily* do any better than those without. Nevertheless, we all know which sort of team we would wish to play in.

Graham Gooch, former captain of Essex and England, said: "It's not vital for a successful side to get on well off the field but it does help. In any walk of life, it's harder to enjoy your work if you don't like your workmates. At Essex, Brian Taylor and then Keith Fletcher instilled the philosophy of enjoying your cricket and being successful at it and we have had a very harmonious dressing room in my time. We have turned down at least one world-class cricketer who wanted to sign for us because we didn't think he would fit in to our particular atmosphere. Neither Doug Insole, Keith Fletcher nor myself would tolerate backbiting among players at our club and if it wasn't sorted out swiftly, their futures at Essex were bleak. It was never all sweetness and light at Essex, though. There were a number of minor skirmishes in the dressing room, and ...two players almost came to blows over a practical joke that went wrong... It can be hard living in each other's pockets for so many days on the trot, month after month, and outbursts of temper are only to be expected occasionally. Every player has his own idiosyncrasies and the secret of a happy dressing room is to accommodate them as long as the rest of the guys can see the point of such tolerance." Graham Gooch, *Captaincy.*

What is the role of the coach in building a harmonious team? At one end of the scale it is his responsibility, in conjunction with the captain, to select the best players who can perform as individuals and still blend into a team. Only in the rarest of instances should the coach have to sacrifice a talented individual in the interests of team cohesiveness.

Teamwork in cricket may well be easier to handle than in many other sports, due to its strong 'socialising' nature. During the season a player will see far more of his team mates than of his family. They are all together in cars or coaches going to a match, in hotels, at meal times, on the field, in the dressing room, and perhaps eating out in the evening. It is unlike football and rugby in that respect. Comparing cricket with football, Bill Athey, formerly of England and Yorkshire, also an ex-professional footballer, but now Head Coach at Worcester, said that after morning training, players would go their own way until the next training session, and thought that might explain the incidence of highly paid young footballers often behaving badly when out on their own in the evenings.

Team spirit can be fostered by harsh criticism – provided that the criticism is deserved. Graham Gooch recalls a test match at Sydney:

> *"We came off the field at the close of play well aware that we might have lost the Test already. We had been bowled out for 152 and they were just fifty– odd behind with nine wickets in hand. England's all-round cricket that day had been poor and our work in the field lethargic. As we plodded off, Mike Hendrick said to no one in particular, "We need a right bollocking – now." Mike Brearley chose the perfect time and tore into us when we walked through the dressing room door. He was so good at things like that. Harsh, angry words from someone usually so calm and collected had an extra significance and they certainly cleared the air. The next day, we bowled and fielded with greater purpose. Then Derek Randall batted for ages in great heat to score 150 and our spinners bowled Australia to defeat."*

## Social loafing

This marvellous phrase may be new to many, but the concept is familiar to all of us, whether active in sport, or in mundane occupations in commerce or industry. Social loafing refers to the fact that individuals in a group do not exert the same effort as they do when working alone. At some level, conscious or otherwise, there is the notion of 'leaving it to the other chap.'

This effect was first noted by a French agricultural engineer, Ringelmann, in the 1890s, when he observed groups pulling on a rope. He realised that the weight that each individual was capable of pulling was not reflected in the pulling power of the group, therefore the individual scores did not add up to the score of the group. He showed that groups of eight did not pull eight times as hard as its individual members, but only four times as hard. In two-man groups, the total pulling power was only 93% of what the individual was capable of pulling. The individual performance decreases as the size of the group increases, and is known as the Ringelmann effect.

Ringelmann's experiments were repeated in the early 1970s and the results obtained were almost identical, the researchers concluding that the lower performance was due to the decrease in motivation, as the group became larger. It was in 1979 when Latine conducted further research that the term 'social loafing' was used. Two years later, further studies led to the conclusion that 'identifiability' was an important ingredient: when individual efforts could not be identified, performance decreased. When they could be identified, social loafing was eliminated.

It would seem that there is no evidence in sport literature to suggest that team selection should be based on anything but individual performance, but as every captain and cricket coach knows this is not as easy as it might seem. In a team sport, the ability to integrate with others is important and individual performances may not reflect this ability. But this brings us full circle, back to the comments in Chapter One, with Nasser Hussain including so-called 'difficult' players, Caddick and Tuffnell, in the England team, his views on this matter being endorsed by the then South African coach, Bob Woolmer who rightly says that it's then up to the captain and coach to make eccentric or difficult players feel part of the team. Was Hussain's confidence in Caddick justified? Well, he did take 7 for 46 in the third Test in 1999 against South Africa and was Wisden Cricketer of the Year.

The coach will be able to make his own 'difficult' players feel part of the team if he focuses on a few of the skills outlined in these chapters.

V.S. Naipaul, celebrated West Indian novelist and Booker prize winner, had this to say in his nineteen-sixties short story, *Test*: -

*"Close, Barrington, Titmus, Shackleton, Trueman, Dexter. Butcher, Worrell, Hall, Griffith, Kanhai, Solomon. Cricket a team game? Teams play, and one team is to be willed to victory. But it is the individual who remains in the memory, he who has purged the emotions by delight and fear."*

# CHECKLIST FOR TEAMWORK

❖ Much of what we know about teamwork in the UK has derived from industrial studies rather than sport.

❖ Dr Meredith Belbin has developed a theory of teamwork that depends for its success on a team having diverse personalities. Nine such team role types have been identified, each having positive characteristics and 'allowable weaknesses.' Many of these team role types may be applicable to a cricket team.

❖ Team cohesion refers to the manner in which team members interact with each other.

❖ There are two aspects of team cohesion: social cohesion and task cohesion. Social cohesion refers to the extent to which team members get along with each other. Task cohesion refers to the extent to which they commit to achieving the team's objectives.

❖ These two ingredients can operate independently so that one can be low and the other high.

❖ Task cohesion is likely to have a positive impact on performance; social cohesion less so.

❖ Within teams, co-operation and competitiveness will co-exist. The degree of co-operation required will vary from one sport to another, with a larger degree of co-operation being required of the smaller team.

❖ Successful teams are high in self-esteem.

❖ Stability is an important element of team cohesion. Team cohesion needs time to develop. On major study put the optimum period for team success at five years.

❖ Our team behaviour can vary dependent on the situation in which we find ourselves.

❖ A degree of contention is likely to be productive within a team providing it can be controlled.

❖ Whilst team cohesiveness is an ideal to aim for, it should not prevent the inclusion of talented if 'difficult' players. They have to be managed.

❖ Social loafing is a phenomenon in which individual effort is diluted when that individual is a member of a team.

# 14   The personality of the cricket coach

*"I imitated other players but never had a word of
coaching.   Without natural ability, therefore,
improvement was meagre.   I visualised clearly the
actions my body ought to perform but it was not well
enough co-ordinated to perform them.   I watched with
amazement a younger and quite ordinary boy dance
down the wicket to drive.   What unjust deity had
conferred such professional ability?"*

From Sparrow Park to Stanley Park
Roy Fuller

On the first Bradford course, we felt it important that we knew as
much as possible about the role of the cricket coach.  We wanted to
look beyond the technical aspects of the job – to find out *how* the
coach dealt with his players.  What sort of coach was likely to be
successful?  A hard-liner, a listener, an authoritarian, a shoulder-to-
cry-on, or none of these?

First, we found that coaches have many different job titles
throughout county cricket, and that apart from the more obvious ones
such as National Coach (although there were several of these),
County Coach and Assistant Coach, there was Head Coach, Cricket
Development Officer and Director of Cricket to name just a few.
Were they all essentially the same job we wondered, but with varying
titles?   In some respects county cricket clubs are autonomous and
have the freedom to call their coaches whatever they deem suitable.

Apart from the technical knowledge of cricket which was a given,
what were the key skills required in a successful coach, and could
we identify them? Were the coach's man management skills very
different from say, those of a manager in industry or commerce?   If
so, in what ways? Was it any easier to manage a team of cricketers,
than say, a section in an office, or a group of people in a manufacturing
organisation?   After all, cricketers were more likely to be highly
motivated than people in an industrial or commercial setting might be
- if only because they were doing what they loved to do - so were
they easier to manage?  And surely those playing cricket for their

167

county – and even for their country – would need little further motivation?

These were just a few of the questions that we sought to resolve.


## Personality

Having decided that we needed to look at the job skills or competencies required of a cricket coach, we then wanted to look at personal characteristics. Did success or the lack of it affect their confidence? Were they anxious? Were they assertive? Were they open to change, or were they more 'traditional' thinkers – after all there is nothing more traditional than cricket, so perhaps it attracted traditional thinkers? We thought they might be extravert, and moderately assertive, confident and relaxed, for example. Was there such a thing, we asked ourselves as a specific 'cricket personality'?

Research into the personalities of athletes in the broad sense of the word, and even of spectators, has been conducted over many years and with a variety of personality assessments, the most frequently used assessment, being Cattell's Sixteen Personality Factor Questionnaire (16PF) (see Appendix 1.) The object of most of these studies has been to determine the key personality characteristics that might lead to competitive success. The personality of an athlete (cricketer) is of interest in its own right, but because of the close link between an athlete and his coach, the characteristics of the coach are of more than passing interest. However there are far fewer studies of sports coaches and none that I know of on first class county cricket coaches.

On a recent course, coaches were given the latest version of the 16PF (Fifth Edition), known as16PF5.

The results were more remarkable for their normality than for anything else, and yet this in itself is intriguing. Of Cattell's sixteen personality factors, fifteen were in the modal 'average' range of 4 – 7. Factor A (Warmth), Factor G (Rule-Consciousness), and Factor $Q_2$ (Self-Reliance), each scored 7, being at the top end of average. Factor $Q_1$ (Openness to Change), was high at 8.

Factor $Q_2$ (Self-Reliance) is interesting. A *low* score would have indicated group-mindedness, cohesiveness, a willingness to be part of a team. The very essence of cricket? Well, in a sense, but we need to remember that it is a team game with a strong focus on individual performance. Some of those attending the course were still playing, maybe coaching minor teams, but were interested in becoming full time coaches when their playing days were over.

Factor $Q_1$ (Openness to Change) is also interesting. There are few games more traditional than cricket. Since attendance on the Bradford course was voluntary, could it be that it attracted those who were keen to improve their coaching skills and were more open to new ideas?

Factor O (Apprehension) is really about levels of confidence. The more confident person scores in the range 1 – 3 and those who are self-doubting, guilt-ridden, and who blame themselves unnecessarily for things that go wrong, score 8 – 10. Would you not expect those who have performed – or are still performing – in front of thousands of people, to be above average in confidence when compared to the average adult British male? It seems that they are not. Are they more emotionally stable than most? It seems not. Are they assertive then? No, this factor came out as average. There are coaching advantages in having a lack of assertiveness of course. People who are less assertive tend to be better listeners, much less concerned at thrusting their own views forward than hearing what others have to say. The coaches' level of general anxiety is no more or less than that of the average British male. More importantly, their level of self-esteem is only average. We know that self-esteem, similar to Bandura's concept of self-efficacy – is an important factor in sporting success. Should their self-esteem not be higher – after all, they are important figures in the cricketing community who have achieved much in their chosen sport? This sense of achievement does not seem to be reflected anywhere in the profile. Leadership potential was, however, slightly higher than average.

## Classification of coaches

At least two sports psychologists have advanced the view that coaches can be classified according to their psychological make-up. These are: *hard-nosed authoritarians*; *nice guys*; *intense* or *driven*; *easygoing*; *business-like*. Although they say that few coaches would fit entirely into one of these categories, "the overriding characteristics usually place coaches in one category or the other." My view is that if we were to classify the cricket coaches in the study mentioned above along these lines, they would be either 'nice guys', or 'easygoing'. Is this a surprise? Not really, because there is a theory that personality can be 'sport specific'. In a large study in the USA, Kroll and Crenshaw used the 16PF to study 387 athletes. This group was made up of 81 footballers, 141 gymnasts, 94 wrestlers, and 71 karate participants. The researchers found that these sportsmen seemed to fall into two groups. The footballers and wrestlers had similar characteristics, and were different from the gymnasts and karate participants. The researchers were surprised to find the footballers and wrestlers having similar characteristics, because whilst the demands of their sport might be similar – strength, agility and endurance - football is a team sport whilst wrestling is individualistic. The gymnasts tended to be intelligent, and relaxed, and had a more serious outlook on life. Karate participants were tense, conscientious, rule-bound and independent.

It does not take a great leap of imagination to believe that cricketers are unlikely to be as aggressive as say, footballers, (although I know of no other research to substantiate this statement.) Therefore we can see that cricket coaches might have been drawn to the game in the first place because they had a 'gut feel' that it suited them, that they were likely to 'fit in'.

There is another point that follows on from this. In the *Psychology of Coaching* Tutko and Ogilvie have suggested that at college level, aggressive coaches tend to pick aggressive players; conservative coaches tend to pick conservative players. This idea seems to be acceptable on a 'common sense' basis. Surely we feel more relaxed when with people who share our values and behave in a roughly similar way? Therefore aren't we more likely to pick those who reflect these attitudes? Perhaps this explains why previous England cricket captains have left out the two players mentioned in Chapter One, and emphasises maybe the more radical approach adopted by Nasser Hussain?

## Tough-mindedness and behaviour

But where does this argument take us in response to current media comment that the England cricket team needs to have more aggression - more mental toughness? A more rugged approach to their game, we are told. By implication this must include cricket coaches. Is this realistic? Can we change the persona of a cricket team, which probably reflects characteristics of the game as played in this country? Cricket fans look to the Australian and South

African sides as exemplars of mental toughness. But they *are* Australian and South African, and there *are* such things as national characteristics. Refer to *When Cultures Collide* by Richard D Lewis (1996) and *Riding the Waves of Culture* by Frons Trompenaars (1997), and you will see what I mean about differing national characteristics. So if the Australian cricket team reflects tougher Australian attitudes, and the England team reflects less competitive English attitudes, are we asking our players to change their personalities? That would seem to be ridiculous.

But wait a minute. Changing their personalities – no. But what about their *behaviour?* Perhaps that could be changed. Recall the point in Chapter Twelve on Leadership, that two American Universities viewed leadership in behavioural terms rather than as a consequence of inborn personality characteristics? Perhaps the answer lies in some conclusions by L B Hendry who studied the personality traits of highly successful American swimming coaches.

## The 'ideal' coach

Forty-eight coaches and thirty-seven swimmers were asked to construct a personality profile for the 'ideal' coach. Both groups agreed that the coach should be "outgoing, dominating, stable, highly intelligent, conscientious, realistic, practical and confidently secure". He should also be "willing to break with tradition, make his own decisions and be very self-sufficient." But where are we likely to find this paragon? And if we can't find him does it mean there are no ideal coaches?

Let's have a look at Hendry's 'ideal' coach again and see how the Bradford cricket coaches compared. On most of the characteristics they were in the average range. That would indicate that they would only need to move two points or so from the centre of the scale to clearly meet Hendry's criteria. They are already showing a willingness to break with tradition and to be self-sufficient.

When the successful swimming coaches were compared to this 'ideal' template, they varied on fourteen of the sixteen traits contained in the 16PF. Hendry concluded *"appropriate role-playing and the possession of materially useful abilities by the coach may be of more use to the swimmers than a particular personality pattern."* (My Italics.) In other words the ability to override one's personality characteristics if necessary, and simulate a certain type of behaviour, may lead to coaching success.

In my own studies with cricket coaches I used ASE's Personal Competency Framework to identify the 'important', and 'very important', skills (as distinct from personality traits), needed in a coach. The consensus was: problem analysis, judgement, technical expertise, listening, motivating others, and resilience. A second study required seventeen cricket coaches to identify very important skills only. They selected judgement, technical expertise, impact, resilience, leading, integrity, stress tolerance, sensitivity, and openness to change. Of these competencies, leading, resilience, stress tolerance, sensitivity and openness to change can be measured with the 16PF5. The cricket coaches scored in the average range for most of these, again showing flexibility of behaviour and we should note the potential value of that to the coach. We can tentatively conclude from this that their actual personality traits are not that far removed from their own conception of the 'ideal'. The cynic might say, "Well they would, wouldn't they?" We need to remember however, that from the coaches' point of view, there was nothing at stake here. When completing the personality assessment the 'impression management' scores (an indicator at to whether the coach was trying to project a markedly favourable impression) were in the mid-range, so distortion was not an issue.

## Return to a 'Golden Age'?

There is of course a counter argument to all this which invokes the glories of a previous age – some might think a golden age – of cricket. Where are the likes of Compton, the Bedser twins, Edrich, Trueman, or Hutton? Bringing it more up to date, where are the Bothams? But the reader might say was there ever really a golden age of cricket?

Peter Wynne-Thomas, cricket historian at Trent Bridge has this to say:

> *"England were slaughtered by Australia in 1946-47.*
> *Bradman came here in 1948 and England were*
> *swamped. Lindwall and Miller were the fast bowlers.*
> *But if there was a Golden Age of post-war cricket it must*
> *have been around the mid- fifties. In the 1950-51 tour,*
> *England beat Australia in the 5th Test but lost the series.*
> *England won the Ashes in 1953, which was around the*
> *end of the Compton era, and about the time that Peter*

> *May, Jim Laker and Bob Appleyard were becoming
> established.   In 1953 Len Hutton became the first
> professional in the 20th century to captain England
> (there had been others in the last century.)  In 1954- 55
> England went to Australia under Hutton and won 3 – 1.
> In 1956 we won again under May.  It was also in 1956
> that Laker took 19 wickets at Old Trafford."*

So are we to conclude that the players of the 1950s had a tougher mental attitude – or were more competitive - than are the players of today, and if so, did this have anything to do with the role of the coach?  Well, England didn't have a coach in those days!  The 1950 - 51 tour was captained by Freddie Brown, and M A Green and J A Nash who both had business experience, acted as managers.  They were not coaches.  The post of England coach is a more recent innovation.

How real is the tough-mindedness of the Australians?  Very real. When they played New Zealand in February 2000 they had a plan of 'controlled aggression'.  The night before the match, the Australian coach slipped the details of their game plan under the wrong doors at their Wellington hotel, and the recipients were New Zealand supporters who quickly gave the details to a local radio station.  The tactics were broadcast before the start of the one-day match.  The comments highlighted weaknesses of various opposition team members and advocated 'the use of controlled aggression to intimidate – but keep sledging and body language under control.'   Did the disclosure of their plans embarrass the Australians?  Certainly, but it didn't stop them achieving 119 – 1 in 23 overs before rain stopped play!

In summary we can say that there have been very few studies of the personality of the successful sports coach, and some of these have been inconclusive.  Both athletes and coaches have their vision of the 'ideal' characteristics that a successful coach should have. Technical knowledge of the sport is still a powerful factor in successful coaching but *when coupled with coaching behaviour that can vary according to the needs of the situation,* this combination is likely to lead to competitive success.

Evidence from the (admittedly small) study at Bradford seems to indicate that personality traits of the cricket coach are 'flexible'.  So if Hendry is correct in saying that 'appropriate behaviour' and the 'possession of materially useful abilities' is important, we can argue that our coaches have an advantage, and by implication, our cricketers. Remember that cricket coaches are drawn from cricketers!  Because they do not appear to have 'entrenched' personality characteristics, they can use the flexibility referred to above to adapt their behaviour accordingly.  At least one club is doing this.  Steve Watkin, a senior player with Glamorgan and a former Test cricketer said:

> *"Our new coach is Geoff Hammond and he's helping us to become more tough-minded.  We've just had a two-day survival course on Brecon Beacons.  It was tough but good fun also.  It was an opportunity for him to get to know us, and for us to bond as a team before the season starts.  If we demonstrate tough-mindedness in our behaviour we'll need to switch it on and off – just as we do with concentration."*

With regard to the managerial style of the coach, Steve said: " *You've got eleven players in the team and each will respond differently. The coach has to understand that.  Our last coach was Duncan Fletcher. He was fairly easy-going but he was* authoritative – *not authoritarian.  I've never come across a really authoritarian coach in cricket"*.

The reader might reasonably question whether it is possible for coaches to adopt the sort of flexible behaviour that seems to be required, and for players to assume the "tough-minded" attitude to cricket that is advocated.  My answer is that we do it all the time! We adopt a certain type of behaviour when meeting clients or customers, with our boss, and when dealing with friends and family. Admittedly, some types of behaviour are more difficult to sustain than are others; we can manage 'interview behaviour' for an hour or so, but may find it difficult to sustain for long periods, and eventually our more 'natural' behaviour might emerge.  Perhaps our behaviour has the properties of an elastic band  - it will eventually return to its original shape.  But our 'parent behaviour' however continues for most of our lives, eventually becoming part of our 'natural' behaviour. When single mothers were monitored in an assessment unit for 24 hours a day on their 'motherhood skills', it was found that they could maintain acceptable behaviour and standards for a period of six weeks. When the assessment period was extended to twelve weeks only those for whom this behaviour came naturally met the high standards required.

So behaviour can be flexible and adjusted within limits to meet specific situations. As Steve Watkin says, there is a parallel here with attentional focus, which we dealt with in Chapter Eight. We saw that attention needs to be switched on and off as required because it could not be sustained indefinitely. So with behaviour.

## Implications for coaching

Given that the behaviour of cricketers and coaches appears to be adaptable, and assuming that a more 'tough-minded' approach is required for cricketing success, what can we do to develop this characteristic? The following are a few suggestions:

1. Training with the use of video. Show examples of cricketers using more extreme behaviours, followed by a discussion of when and why the adoption of such behaviours might be helpful.
2. Training by anecdotal evidence. Review of past examples of when the coach was unable to successfully influence a player's behaviour, and the strategies the coach might have adopted that could have been more successful.
3. Try using role-play techniques which allow coaches to 'try out' alternative behaviours.

If it is correct, as my work with cricket coaches seems to suggest, that coaches and players have somewhat flexible personality characteristics, then we need to capitalise on this.

Perhaps Mike Hendrick had this in mind when he told me with admirable brevity at the 1999 World Cup Cricket Coaches' Conference, "The coach needs to be versatile."

# CHECK LIST - PERSONALITY OF THE CRICKET COACH

❖ A small study of the personalities of professional cricket coaches showed that on most characteristics they scored around the average for adult British males.

❖ The result of a skills analysis showed that coaches needed to be problem solvers, to have good judgement, to be technically competent, good listeners, good motivators, and to be resilient.

❖ These last three factors can be obtained directly or indirectly from 16PF5. The personality profiles in the second study showed that the coaches had no marked tendency to display these characteristics but their 'average' scores indicated a flexibility that would allow them to adopt a more 'tough-minded' stance where appropriate.

❖ Some sport psychologists have classified coaches as being either hard-nosed authoritarians; nice guys; intense or driven; easygoing, or business-like.

❖ Some psychologists believe that there is a 'sport specific' personality.

❖ If this is so, there is some evidence to indicate that cricket coaches might be "nice guys" or "easygoing".

❖ It seems that British cricket coaches and perhaps cricketers, lack the 'mental toughness' often advocated as essential, but this does not explain successes at Test match level in previous decades, particularly the 1950s.

❖ Nevertheless, it seems that successful cricket coaches need a 'kitbag' of behavioural styles to match specific competitive situations and to deal appropriately with individual cricketers.

❖ Technical expertise and the ability to adopt an appropriate behavioural style are more likely to lead to coaching success, than reliance on a particular set of personality traits.

# APPENDIX 1 - The sixteen personality factor questionnaire (16PF5) profile sheet

**PRIMARY FACTORS**

| Factor | Raw | Sten | Left Meaning | Standard Ten Score (STEN) 1–10 | Right Meaning |
|---|---|---|---|---|---|
| A: Warmth | | | More Emotionally Distant from People | | Attentive and Warm to Others |
| B: Reasoning | | | Fewer Reasoning Items Correct | | More Reasoning Items Correct |
| C: Emotional Stability | | | Reactive, Emotionally Changeable | | Emotionally Stable, Adaptive |
| E: Dominance | | | Deferential, Cooperative, Avoids Conflict | | Dominant, Forceful |
| F: Liveliness | | | Serious, Cautious, Careful | | Lively, Animated, Spontaneous |
| G: Rule-Consciousness | | | Expedient, Non-conforming | | Rule-Conscious, Dutiful |
| H: Social Boldness | | | Shy, Threat-Sensitive, Timid | | Socially Bold, Venturesome, Thick-Skinned |
| I: Sensitivity | | | Objective, Unsentimental | | Subjective, Sentimental |
| L: Vigilance | | | Trusting, Unsuspecting, Accepting | | Vigilant, Suspicious, Sceptical, Wary |
| M: Abstractedness | | | Grounded, Practical, Solution-Oriented | | Abstracted, Theoretical, Idea-Oriented |
| N: Privateness | | | Forthright, Straightforward | | Private, Discreet, Non-Disclosing |
| O: Apprehension | | | Self-Assured, Unworried | | Apprehensive, Self-Doubting, Worried |
| Q1: Openness to Change | | | Traditional, Values the Familiar | | Open to Change, Experimenting |
| Q2: Self-Reliance | | | Group-Oriented, Affiliative | | Self-Reliant, Individualistic |
| Q3: Perfectionism | | | Tolerates Disorder, Unexacting, Flexible | | Perfectionistic, Organized, Self-Disciplined |
| Q4: Tension | | | Relaxed, Placid, Patient | | Tense, High Energy, Impatient, Driven |

**GLOBAL FACTORS**

| Factor | | | Left Meaning | Average 1–10 | Right Meaning |
|---|---|---|---|---|---|
| EX: Extraversion | | | Introverted, Socially Inhibited | | Extraverted, Socially Participating |
| AX: Anxiety | | | Low Anxiety, Unperturbed | | High Anxiety, Perturbable |
| TM: Tough-Mindedness | | | Receptive, Open-Minded | | Tough-Minded, Resolute |
| IN: Independence | | | Accommodating, Agreeable, Selfless | | Independent, Persuasive, Wilful |
| SC: Self-Control | | | Unrestrained, Follows Urges | | Self-Controlled, Inhibits Urges |

## PRIMARY FACTORS

| Low score (1-3) | Average (4-7) | High score (8-10) |
|---|---|---|
| **A: Warmth**<br>Less inclined to seek personal involvement. Tends to be more detached. | Shows an average level of warmth towards others. | Has a genuine, warm interest in people. Seeks close relationships. |
| **B: Reasoning**<br>Fewer reasoning items answered correctly. | Average number of reasoning items correct. | More reasoning items correct. |
| **C: Emotional Stability**<br>Generally deals less calmly with life's demands. Changeable in mood. | Deals with life's demands and controls moods to same extent as most people. | Tends to adjust to the facts of the situation, realistic about self and world and generally deals more calmly with life's demands than most people. |
| **E: Dominance**<br>More likely to accommodate to others' wishes and to avoid conflict. Likely to make fewer demands. | Likely to express views and state opinions whilst being assertive rather than aggressive and willing to defer lead when appropriate. | Tends to be forceful, eager to take the lead and be in control. May be less tolerant of contrary views. |
| **F: Liveliness**<br>More likely to exercise caution and less likely to seek variety. Takes life seriously and anticipates difficulties. | Likely to think things through and exercise caution to same extent as most. Typical need for excitement and variety. | Lively and enthusiastic, may not always fully think things through. Cheerful and happy-go-lucky. |
| **G: Rule-Consciousness**<br>Less likely to be bound by rules and regulations. Improvising and expedient. | Reasonably dutiful and guided by morals to a typical extent. | Likely to feel a strong obligation to follow rules and regulations. |
| **H: Social Boldness**<br>Less at ease socially, prefers stability and predictable environments. | Averagely socially confident. | More at ease socially than most. |
| **I: Sensitivity**<br>Makes decisions based on objective observations. Values the tangible, practical and possible. | Incorporates both subjective and objective viewpoints when evaluating issues. | Judgement usually influenced by subjectivity. Interested in the cultural facets of life. |
| **L: Vigilance**<br>Tends to be trusting, easygoing, and cooperative. Takes people at face value. | Likely to be aware of any real grounds for scepticism but not overly suspicious. | Questions motives of others even when there is no apparent reason for doubt. Less likely to take people at face value. Expects to be misunderstood. |
| **M: Abstractedness**<br>Prefers factual data, adapts to routine easily, pays attention to detail. | Tends to shift easily between facts and theories when processing information. | Reflective, focusing less on detail and more on the broader issues. Less attentive to detail. |
| **N: Privateness**<br>Forthright, less guarded, uncomplicated and natural. | Likely to be as open and self-disclosive as most people. | Less easily reveals information about self. More private and guarded. |
| **O: Apprehension**<br>Less self-critical with higher self-esteem. Feels worthy of love and respect. Confident, relaxed and resilient. | Accepts responsibility for mistakes without being overly self-critical. | More self-critical with lower self-esteem. May be sensitive to criticism from others. Prone to self-blame. |
| **Q₁: Openness to Change**<br>Prefers to maintain established methods, dislikes unfamiliarity. Cautious when considering new ideas. | Values traditional ideas and beliefs whilst remaining open to appropriate and useful change. | Seeks purposeful change. Interested in new ideas. |
| **Q₂: Self-Reliance**<br>Likes to feel a sense of belonging. Prefers to work as part of a team and consult others when making decisions. | Averagely self-sufficient but values a sense of belonging as much as most. | Self-sufficient, preferring to make independent decisions. Values freedom and privacy, tends to concentrate on task as opposed to people. |
| **Q₃: Perfectionism**<br>Less concerned with planning and organizing. Leaves more things to chance. | Organizes and plans ahead to same extent as most. | Highly defined personal standards. Organized and self-disciplined. Wants to do things correctly. |
| **Q₄: Tension**<br>Lower level of physical tension, easy going. Generally satisfied. | Experiences typical levels of physical tension. | High level of physical tension. Could be restless and impatient. |
| **Impression Management**<br>Fewer socially desirable responses. | Self-presentation is not notably favourable or unfavourable. | More socially desirable responses. |

# APPENDIX 2 - Belbin's nine team roles

| Roles and descriptions-<br>team-role contribution | Allowable weaknesses |
| --- | --- |
| **Plant:** Creative, imaginative, unorthodox. Solves difficult problems. | Ignores details. Too pre-occupied to comunicate effectively. |
| **Resource investigator:** Extrovert, enthusiastic, communicative. Explores opportunities. Develops contacts. | Overoptomistic. Loses interest once initial enthusiasm has passed. |
| **Co-ordinator:** Mature, confident, a good chairperson. Clarifies goals, promotes decision-making, delegates well. | Can be see as manipulative. Delegates personal work. |
| **Shaper:** Challenging, dynamic, thrives on pressure. Has the drive and courage to overcome obstacles. | Can provoke others. Hurts people's feelings. |
| **Monitor evaluator:** Sober, strategic and discerning. Sees all options. Judges accurately. | Lacks drive and ability to inspire others. Overly critical. |
| **Teamworker:** Co-operative, mild, perceptive and diplomatic. Listens, builds, averts friction, calms the waters. | Indecisive in crunch situations. Can be easily influenced. |
| **Implementer:** Disciplined, reliable, conservative and efficient. Turns ideas into practical actions. | Somewhat inflexible. Slow to respond to new possibilities. |
| **Completer:** Painstaking, conscientious, anxious. Searches out errors and ommissions. Delivers on time. | Inclined to worry unduly. Reluctant to delegate. Can be a nit-picker. |
| **Specialist:** Single-minded, self-starting, dedicated. Provides knowledge and skills in rare supply. | Contributes on only a narrow front. Dwells on technicalities. Overlooks the 'big picture'. |

# APPENDIX 3 - Communication between the coach and players

## Key points raised at a group discussion of cricket coaches at the Management Centre, Bradford University, January 2000

This discussion centred on Bob Woolmer's proposal that there should be radio contact between the coach and players during the course of play. Coaches at all levels are likely to discuss this issue in the coming seasons as technology increasingly becomes part of our everyday life: the following are some of the pros and cons.

Coaches were asked to discuss:

- The principle of radio contact during play
- The likely effect upon the style of coaching and the role of the coach, if it becomes standard practice
- Whether other coaches would follow Bob Woolmer's lead
- Whether players would welcome such an innovation?

The group consisted of Tim Boon, (national coach); John Emburey, (independent coach); Mick Newell (Nottinghamshire); Steve Rhodes (Worcestershire); Tony Wright (Gloucestershire),

- Do you really want a coach to tell you what to do?
- How are young boys going to work it out for themselves if the coach is interfering?
- The player is experiencing problems *now* – out in the middle. With 15 – 19 year olds, you can advise them in the dressing room, but out in the middle they forget it.
- The coach's job is to *prepare* players, not play the game for them.
- At what point should the coach's job stop?
- Players need to develop a cricketing brain.
- Players should learn from those around them – particularly the captain and the vice-captain.
- If it is to be used, would that be at Test, county, or local level?
- What about using it only in practice?  It might be OK in the nets.
- It would be useful at junior level but not senior level.

- Could lead to players being reliant on someone other than themselves.
- To learn, you have to make mistakes, and experience them yourself.
- The coach may do less coaching before the game, because in effect he will be in charge of the game.
- It would undermine the authority of the captain. It would dilute the responsibility and power of the captain.
- Although football coaches talk to players from the touchline, a cricket captain has more responsibility compared to a football captain, who is largely a figurehead.
- Might be OK in international cricket and with junior players.
- Should it finally be the players' decision?

# APPENDIX 4 - Key characteristics of a 'good' captain and a 'bad' captain

## *'GOOD' CAPTAIN*

| *SITUATION* | *ACTION/BEHAVIOUR* |
|---|---|
| 1<br>Team not doing well. | Remained calm.<br>Totally in control.<br>Gave praise.<br>Ignored weaknesses.<br>Obviously enjoyed the game.<br>Relaxed manner – transferred to others. |
| 2<br>Trouble with run-up during match.<br>Bowling with the wind, resulted in no-balls, lack of rhythm. | Sought advice of senior bowler.<br>Told to bowl into wind.<br>Took advice.<br>Valued players' opinions. |
| 3<br>Team needs a plan for a run of 1-day (50 over competition). | Captain planned. Communicated a practical plan to the team .<br>Mutual trust/respect with players.<br>Excellent man-management.<br>Team won 8 out of 8 matches. |
| 4<br>Team were 50 – 4 in Lord's final of B & H cup. Sunday rained off.<br>"We'll win this on Monday, make sure you are ready to come back and win. | Instilled belief in batsmen that we would win. Confidence high - team won.<br>Led from front.<br>Players wanted to prove they could play.<br>Goals, tactics, work rate, self-belief. |
| 5<br>Batsman having a bad time. Playing OK but getting out. Expected to be dropped. | Spent 3-½ hrs with batsman instilling confidence. |

| SITUATION | ACTION/BEHAVIOUR |
|---|---|
| 6<br>Game plans for one day cricket. | Showed faith in players.<br>Intuitive.<br>Good communicator.<br>Kept things simple.<br>Set clear goals. |
| 7<br>Inherited very weak side. | Inspirational (strong personality)<br>Conscientious. Good communicator.<br>Trust. Acted as captain - not just w/k and batter. Captain does not have to be best performer. |
| 8<br>Occasional days as captain Demonstrated leadership in most situations. | Inspirational. Attacking and positive.<br>Had players' respect.<br>Gave confidence to players.<br>Willing you to succeed.<br>Took lead in difficult situations.<br>Inspirational. Imaginative, attacking, positive. Good influence on players.<br>Believed in his own limited ability.<br>Instilled confidence in players.<br>Willing you to succeed. |
| 9<br>Planned changes.<br>Swopped fielders. | Never let batters settle.<br>Authoritative. Brave. Loyal. |
| 10<br>In most situations showed the following characteristics. | Organised. Astute. Realistic.<br>Knowledge of the game.<br>Earned respect. Humorous. |
| 11<br>"Never allowed opposition to settle." | Good communicator.<br>Showed respect.<br>Tactical problem solver. |

| SITUATION | ACTION/BEHAVIOUR |
| --- | --- |
| 12 | Open mind; Led from front. Father figure. Tough. Resourceful. Can turn negative into positive. |
| 13 Generally... | Communicator with all players. Works hard. Puts himself out. Problem solver. Listener. |

# 'BAD' CAPTAIN

| SITUATION | ACTION/BEHAVIOUR |
|---|---|
| **1**<br>Team had run of bad results. | Wrapped up in himself.<br>Forgets the team. |
| **2**<br>Was not number one bowler as was usually the case. | Bad body language.<br>No communication or support.<br>No discussion of reasons behind decisions. |
| **3**<br>B & H game. Had won 4 out of 4.<br>No game plan for the 5th game.<br>All out for low score. Pitch turned and bounced but spinner didn't bowl. | Captain didn't bowl the right players. |
| **4**<br>Dropped a player 10 mins before match. Vague excuses. Didn't want to chat it over after game. | Bad communiccation.<br>Didn't ask for advice.<br>Loner. |
| **5**<br>Young player dropped two catches. | Captain shouted at player across the ground. |
| **6**<br>Test match. | Captain declared when key player was on 96.<br>Bad influence on team – put team in low mood.<br>Ignored affect on morale. |
| **7**<br>Captain of 3 years attracted ex-international players and younger players were peaking. | Tell, tell, tell!<br>No encouragement.<br>His large ego alienated many people. Selfish.<br>Allowed cliques to develop. |

| SITUATION | ACTION/BEHAVIOUR |
|---|---|
| 8<br>Team of hard players to manage. | False praise. Lack of trust and respect for him as a captain and a person. Economical with the truth. Bully. Demonstrative and loud. Poor leader and influence. Had been a good vice–captain. |
| 9<br>Did not show character, guts or determination when needed. | Happy to be on fringe.<br>Would not get stuck in.<br>Nice guy but not cut out to be captain. |
| 10<br>Would not confront players when needed. | Poor communicator.<br>Lacked humour. |
| 11<br>Players bag thrown out of dressing room for fun. | Predictable.<br>Used the wrong words at the wrong time.<br>"What's wrong with you, you bastard." |
| 12<br>Captain avoided tough decisions –<br>"We'll talk about it later." | Weak leadership. |
| 13<br>Told player he wasn't playing 5 mins before match.<br>Confusion between coach and captain. | Political reasons for non-selection.<br>Poor communicator. |

# References

## Chapter 1  Interpreting Other's Behaviour

1       Cattell, R.B., *The Sixteen Personality Factor Questionnaire*, Institute of Personality and Ability Testing Inc., Champaign, Illinois.  Published in the UK by ASE, a division of NFER – NELSON Publishing Company, Ltd.
2       Jung C. G., (1923) *Psychological Types,* tr. H.G. Baynes, London.

## Chapter 2  Presenting Yourself

1       Goffman, E., (1959) *The Presentation of Self in Everyday Life.* Anchor Books, USA.
2       Wainwright, G., (1985) *Body Language,* Hodder Headline plc.
3       Burne, J., quoted in *Body and Mind*, Financial Times, 11th - 12th March 2000.

## Chapter 3  Motivation

1       Fisher, A.C. (1976) *Psychology of Sport,* Mayfield Publishing Co, Palo Alto, Ca.,
2       Woodworth, A.S. and Schlosberg, H.  (1954) *Experimental Psychology.* Revised  Edition, New York: Holt Rinehart and Winston.
3       Siedentopp, D., and Ramey, G., *Extrinsic rewards and intrinsic motivation. Motor Skills:* Theory into Practice, 2, 49 – 62.
4       McGregor, D., (1960) *The Human Side of Enterprise.* McGraw-Hill, NY.
5       Carling, W., and Heller, R., (1995) *The Way to Win,* Little, Brown and Co.
6       Dick, F. Seminar at World Cricket Coaches Conference and Exhibition, N.E.C., Birmingham, 1st June 1999.

## Chaper 4 Attribution

1    Heider, F., (1958) *The Psychology of Interpersonal Relations.* NY. Wiley.
2    Weiner, B., (1974) *Achievement Motivation and Attribution Theory.* Morristown, NJ., General Learning Press.
3    Rotter, J.B., (1971) *External Control and Internal Control.* Psychology Today, pp 37 – 42.
4    Dweck, C., (1975) *The role of expectations and attributions in the alleviation of learned helplessness.* Journal of Personality and Social Psychology, **31**, 674 – 685.

## Chapter 5  Arousal, Stress and Anxiety

1    Yerkes, R.M., and Dodson, J.D., (1908) *The relationship of strength of stimulus to rapidity of habit formation.* Journal of comparative Neurology and Psychology, 18, 459 – 482.
2    Horn T.S.  (1992) *Advances in Sport Psychology.* Human Kinetics Publishers. Champaign, Illinois.
3    Lord  W. (1997) 16PF5 – *Personality in Practice.* NFER-NELSON.
4    Davies D. and Armstrong M. (1989) *Psychological Factors in Competitive Sport,* The Falmer Press.

## Chapter 6  Relaxation

1    Fontana D.  (1990)  *Managing Stress.*  The British Psychological Society and  Routledge Ltd.
2    Benson, H., Kotch, J.B.,  Crassweller K.D., and Greenwood, M.M.,(1977) *Historical and clinical considerations of the relaxation response.* American Scientist. **65,** 441 – 443.
3    Harris D.V. & Harris B.L (1984) *The athlete's guide to sports psychology: Mental skills for physical people.* Leisure Press. Champaign, Illinois.

## Chapter 7  Mental Rehearsal

1    Nicklaus J., (1974) *Golf My Way.* New York. Simon and Schuster.
2    Hemery, D. (1986) *The Pursuit of Sporting Excellence.* Human Kinetics Books, Champaign, Illinois.

3    Syer J and Connolly C (1984) *Sporting Body, Sporting Mind: An Athlete's Guide to Mental Training.* Cambridge University Press.

4    Quoted by Andrew Derrington, Professor of Psychology, University of Nottingham, in Psych Yourself Up, Financial Times, 20/21 Nov 1999.

5    Horn T. (1992) (Editor). *Advances in Sport Psychology.* Human Kinetics Publishers Inc.

6    Adapted from Hickman, J.L.., (1979) How to elicit supernormal capabilities in athletes. In P. Klavora and J.V. Daniel (editors) *Coach, athlete and sport psychologist.* Human Kinetics publishers, Champaign, Il.

## Chapter 8  Attentional Focus and Style

1    Hemery, D. (1986) *The Pursuit of Sporting Excellence.*

2    Ibid.

3    Nideffer, R.M., (1976) *The Inner Athlete.* New York: Crowell

4    Ibid.

5    Crace, J and Smith, R., (1992) *Quest for Number One,* BPCC Hazell Books Ltd.

## Chapter Nine  Self Efficacy

1    Morris T. and Summers J. (1995)  *Sport Psychology: Theory, Applications, and Issues.*   J Wiley.

2    Bandura A.  (1977) *Self-Efficacy:* Toward a unifying theory of behaviour change. *Psychological Review, 84 191 – 215.*

## Chapter Ten Oral Communication

1    Carling W. and Heller R. (1995) *The Way to Win.* Little, Brown and Co.

2    Gleeson G.R. (1967).  *Judo for the West.* Kaye and Ward Ltd.

## Chapter Eleven Active Listening

1    Mackay, I., (1995) *Listening Skills,* 2$^{nd}$ Edition, IPD.

## Chapter Twelve Leadership

1    Carron, A.V., (1989) *Social Psychology of Sport.* Ithaca. NY Mouvemont Publications)
2    McGregor, D., (1960) *The Human Side of Enterprise,* McGraw-Hill.
3    Blake, R.R., and Mouton, J.S., (1978) *The New Managerial Grid.* Houston, TX, Gulf Publishing Company.
4    Fiedler, F.E., (1967) *A theory of leadership effectiveness.* NY. McGraw-Hill.
5    Carron, A.V., (1980) *Social Psychology of Sport..* Ithaca. NY Mouvemont Publications.
6    Hersey, P., and Blanchard, K., (1969) Life cycle theory of leadership. *Training and Development Journal,* 23, 26 – 34.

## Chapter Thirteen Teamwork

1    Belbin  R. Meredith. (1981) *Management Teams: Why they succeed or fail.* Heinemann Professional Publishing Ltd.
2    Carron, A. V., (1982) Cohesiveness in sport groups: Interpretations and considerations. *Journal of Sport Psychology, 4, 123 – 138.*
3    Belbin R. Meredith (1993). *Team Roles at Work.* Butterworth-Heinemann Ltd.
4    Pascale, R., (1982) *The Art of Japanese Management.* London, Allen Lane. Originally published in NY, Simon and Schuster, 1981.
5    Kauss, D.R., (1980) *Peak Performance,* Prentice-Hall.

# INDEX

# C

## D

## E

## F

# G

# H

# I

# J

# K

# L

# M

# S

# Y

# Z